AF594663

A NEW HISTORY OF

LEXINGTON, KENTUCKY

FOSTER OCKERMAN JR.

THE History PRESS

Published by The History Press
Charleston, SC
www.historypress.com

Copyright © 2021 by Foster Ockerman Jr.
All rights reserved

The first version of this history was published as *Historic Lexington, Heart of the Bluegrass* by Lammert Inc., which retains the copyright to the original work. Material therefrom is used by permission of Lammert Inc.

Manufactured in the United States

ISBN 9781467146852

Library of Congress Control Number: 2021943429

Notice: The information in this book is true and complete to the best of our knowledge. It is offered without guarantee on the part of the author or The History Press. The author and The History Press disclaim all liability in connection with the use of this book.

All rights reserved. No part of this book may be reproduced or transmitted in any form whatsoever without prior written permission from the publisher except in the case of brief quotations embodied in critical articles and reviews.

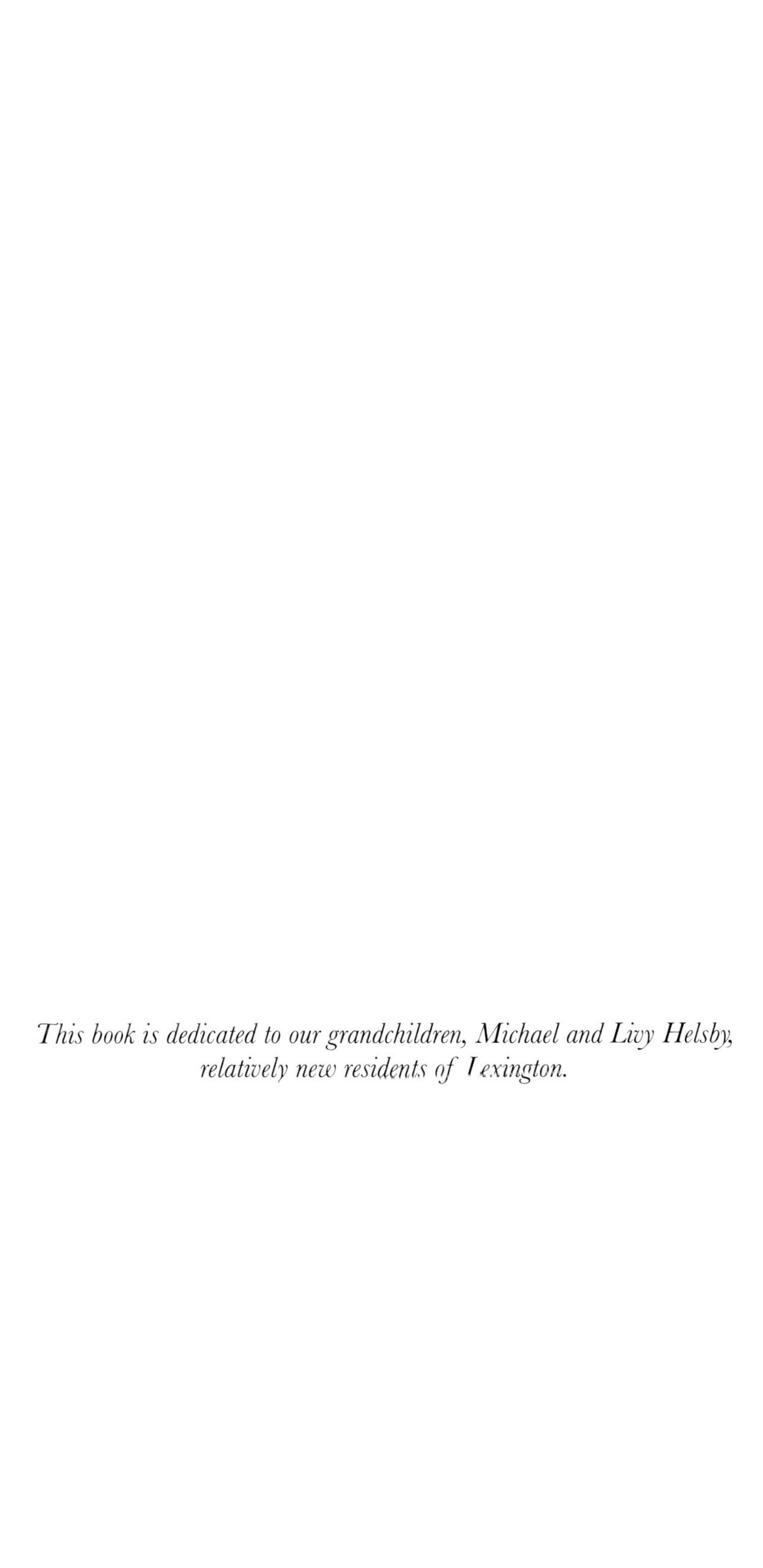

This book is dedicated to our grandchildren, Michael and Livy Helsby, relatively new residents of Lexington.

CONTENTS

ACKNOWLEDGEMENTS

I want to thank the Lexington History Museum Inc. for sponsoring the publication of the first edition of this history in 2013 and Lammert Inc., the original publisher, for granting permission to use material from that first edition for a relatively modest sum. Thanks, as always, to Sarah Hubbard and her staff at the Kentucky Room of the Lexington Public Library for their helpful assistance and to fellow historian William M. Ambrose for sharing some of his privately published books. I appreciated the cooperation of libraries at the University of Kentucky in providing access to unpublished manuscripts during a period of a general shutdown of research facilities during the early stages of the pandemic. And a special gratitude to my wife, Martina, for her love and support during this time of COVID seclusion and for allowing me once again to make a forced occupation of the table in our new kitchen to spread out my notes and prepare the manuscript.

INTRODUCTION

The history of Lexington begins with water: water that evaporated from an ancient inland sea, leaving salt licks to attract bison in vast herds that made the first trails; water that flows through the limestone strata to provide the foundation for strong horses; water, bubbling clear from abundant springs into streams and rivers to attract game and sustain grasslands where Native Americans hunted for centuries; water that attracted settlers to follow the bison trails and build cabins and forts and communities; water, filtered through limestone, that became an essential ingredient in fine Kentucky bourbon. Lexington's history with water is reflected in the names of its streets and roads: Spring Street, Water Street (running along Town Branch), Grimes Mill Road and Clays Mills Road, for example.

At the waters of McConnell's Spring, a group of men decided to establish the town of Lexington.

Prior to 1772, what would become Lexington lay in Botetourt County, Virginia, a large expanse of land encompassing what is today western Virginia, Kentucky and parts of Illinois, Indiana, Ohio and West Virginia, extending the colony of Virginia's claims to the Mississippi River. In that year, Botetourt County—named for the popular royal governor, Lord Botetourt—was divided, and the future central Kentucky became part of the new Fincastle County, evidently named for Lord Botetourt's English home.

By 1776, however, revolutionary fervor had begun to influence the Virginia legislature. Botetourt's successor as governor, John Murry, Earl of Dunmore and Viscount of Fincastle, was leading the military opposition.

Town Branch. *Katrina Ockerman.*

Fincastle County was abolished. Its area was divided into three counties: Washington, Montgomery and Kentucky, the latter comprising roughly the current boundaries of the state.

This is more than a recitation of political and geographical history. It is evidence of expanding population in the western lands. The county is a state administrative unit with a court, justices of the peace, a sheriff, militias and other public officers and administrative functions. When Kentucky County was divided into three counties in 1780, the act passed by the Virginia legislature recited the "great inconveniences for the want of due administration of justice, arising principally from the great extent of the county and the dispersed situation of the settlements" as the grounds for action. The three counties thus created were Fayette, Jefferson and Lincoln.

Lexington was designated as the county seat for Fayette County and its court given jurisdiction for "all actions and suits in law and equity" then pending in the former Kentucky County. Louisville and Harrodsburg were the other new county seats. The Fayette County surveyor was directed to pick a county for his office and deliver to the two new surveyors all entries claiming land for which there was not yet a survey. For each of these entries he would be paid three pounds of tobacco.

1

NATIVE AMERICANS IN KENTUCKY

The Treaty of Paris in 1763 ended the French and Indian War, as the colonists called it—since that is who they fought. It was known in Europe as the Seven Years' War among the major powers, including England, France and Spain.

According to the terms of the treaty, France surrendered its claims in North America on lands east of the Mississippi River to England and to Spain for those to the west. England's King George III immediately drew a Line of Demarcation along the crests of the Allegheny Mountains, prohibiting any of his subjects along the Atlantic coast from crossing the mountains. His reasons were partly economic (the war had been expensive and he didn't want to incur any more military costs), partly political (the various colonies had conflicting claims to the western lands) and partly strategic (to divert expansion of the colonial population north toward Nova Scotia and south toward Florida along the Atlantic coast to better secure the East Coast). He had little interest in internal development or in starting new wars with Native Americans. The king wanted to restrict occupancy to the coast in order to increase coastal trade among the colonies and with England. That, of course, did not deter adventurous men from probing the mountain ranges, looking for a way through.

The precolonial history of Native Americans in the region is rich and deep and not often explored in popular histories. To begin, two particular myths need to be debunked, however dear to the hearts of Kentucky children who were taught them: 1) the word *Kentucky* is not "Indian" for "dark and bloody ground," and 2) no tribes ever lived in Kentucky, only hunted and fought there. There was and is, of course, no one Native American language, and several tribes were active in Kentucky and Tennessee during our frontier period. In March 1775, Daniel Boone and others acting for the Transylvania Company negotiated with the Chickamauga Cherokee tribal leaders to purchase a large area of land comprising what is now the central and eastern parts of Kentucky and Tennessee. One leader, Chief Dragging Canoe, opposed the sale. He threatened to make the land a "dark and bloody ground" if any white attempted to settle there and left the conference. A treaty was eventually concluded, but it was negated by the legislatures of Virginia and North Carolina. Both states claimed the land. Native Americans living in Kentucky are described in the following sections.

The true original meaning of *kentucky* in its various spellings has not been determined, but a strong contender is the Iroquois word *kentaki*, which means "place of level land" or "place of meadows." It is believed to have been the place name for where the Iroquois village of Eskippakithiki was located in the southeast corner of present-day Clark County. Daniel Boone and other early adventurers picked up the name and applied it more generally to the rolling lands of the Bluegrass Region, certainly full of meadows and level compared to the mountains over which they had climbed and from which they descended into central Kentucky.

Pre-Columbian

Peoples entered what is now Kentucky more than 11,500 years ago. The Clovis, known for their distinctive spear points, were first. Their points featured fluted chipped rock heads. The Clovis were hunter-gathers who lived in extended family groups of one to two dozen and moved across an area. They hunted the megafauna of the time, mastodons and mammoths, as well as smaller game. Related family groups formed loose economic and social ties. Their period ended roughly 8000 BC.

Archaic

For the next two thousand years, the Archaic peoples lived in Kentucky. Like their ancestors, they were nomads and hunter-gathers, but the nature of the game they hunted had changed. They also began experimenting with growing their own crops. Some groups began to settle, making camps by streams and in caves. Axes appeared at this time, as did woven baskets, mats and fishnets.

Woodland Period

The Adena culture, roughly 500 BC to AD 200, found family groups clustering into clans and building semipermanent settlements. The hunters did move seasonally to follow game, but farming or gardening was more prevalent. They also maintained extended relations and trading routes with other tribes. Famously, the Adena built burial mounts for certain of their dead, believed to have been important political, war or religious leaders. The Adena also used herbal medicines to treat maladies and made pottery tempered with native limestone and sometimes decorated with geometric designs.

Fort Ancient Peoples

The Fort Ancient period stretched from AD 900 to 1750, chiefly in central and eastern Kentucky. While still engaged in hunting game and gathering native plants, the Fort Ancient built permanent villages. The earlier villages tended to be rings of small houses around a central plaza. Storage pits were next to each house. After about 1400, or about the time Columbus "discovered" the Americas, the villages grew in size, sometimes housing up to five hundred people. Their arrows were now tipped with flint heads, and other tools such as scrapers, knives and drills were made from chert. Potters made an extensive variety of bowls, pitchers and jars. Personal ornaments of bone and shell were frequent. The old trading networks were extended, and not long after the Jamestown and Plymouth settlements in the early 1600s, metal objects of European origin began filter into the villages.

Historic Period

The historic period in Kentucky is generally considered to begin in 1750 with the discovery of the Cumberland Gap in the mountains by Dr. Thomas Walker, which marked the first relatively easy route from Virginia into the area. The Wilderness Road was blazed from the gap through into central

Kentucky to end at present-day Danville. The Limestone Road, named for a settlement on the Ohio River (present-day Maysville), led south toward what became Lexington. (Limestone Street, a north–south axis through Lexington's downtown, takes its name from this road.) As the English settlers began to infiltrate Kentucky, several tribes lived in parts of Kentucky and defended against the intrusions. The Shawnee lived and hunted in central Kentucky, maintaining a string of villages along the Kentucky side of the Ohio River. They were the most prominent players in opposing the colonists. The Chickasaw fought to retain western Kentucky, while the Chickamauga Cherokee defended their lands in south-central Kentucky and Tennessee. The Miami, Mingo and Wyandot tribes also fought in the war for Kentucky. During the French and Indian War, both the English and the French enlisted Native Americans to fight. During the Revolutionary War, the British, from their bases in Canada, stirred up tribes to attack the growing Kentucky settlements. Again in the War of 1812, England mounted attacks into Kentucky, leading Native American forces. In between those wars, the tribes make life unsettling for the new arrivals.

The last Native American settlement of any significance was the village of Eskippakithiki in the southeast corner of what is today Clark County, where the Bluegrass Region gives rise to the mountains of eastern Kentucky. The Iroquois tribe, which settled there in roughly 1718, called the area kentaki, or "land of meadows." The name would be attached to the nearby river and eventually the entire state. The village name means "place of blue licks" in reference to the salt licks in the area. A salt or mineral lick was an exposed deposit of salt and other minerals needed by animals. They would literally lick the ground to get the salt and made trails from one lick to another. Indians and frontiersmen easily followed these paths hunting the animals, so it was natural for a settlement to be made near both the licks and the Kentucky River. A French census in 1736, while that nation still claimed the area, found two hundred men lived in the village; with women and children, the population could have been four hundred or more. The village was attacked in 1754 by a war party of Ottowa Indians and appears to have been abandoned shortly thereafter. The Iroquois are believed to have traveled north to join a string of Iroquois settlements along the Ohio River in southern Ohio. Various tribes continued to hunt in Kentucky, but the age of residence was almost over.

Some Specific Instances of Attacks

On December 22, 1769, Daniel Boone and members of his hunting party were attacked and captured by Shawnee. After being relieved of their furs and supplies, the men were released with the warning never to return or "the wasps and yellow jackets would sting them." The threat had little effect, and Boone and his men stayed in the area. They were soon captured again but escaped.

In 1771, Boone and his hunters were attacked and robbed by Cherokee. Later in the year, Boone had several encounters with Native Americans.

The year 1776, in which revolution consumed the coastal colonies, saw a different struggle in central Kentucky. In April, the small village of Leestown, near present-day Frankfort on the Kentucky River, was attacked. The survivors abandoned the village and fled to Fort Harrod. In May, Boonesboro was attacked by Shawnee, and two settlers died. They returned in July, this time capturing three girls, including Boone's daughter. Boone led a force to rescue the girls. On Christmas Day, Colonel John Todd, Mary Todd Lincoln's great-uncle, led an attack against the Mingo at Royal Springs. Four days later, the Mingo retaliated with an attack on McClelland's fort there. Several died on each side, and with the death of Chief Pluggy, the Mingo retreated.

As the War for American Independence began, the British tried to exert some degree of control over their Native American allies, offering larger rewards for live prisoners versus the reward for scalps, with varying degrees of success. A friendly visit by the peace-favoring Shawnee Chief Blackfish ended in his murder, which enraged that tribe. A planned invasion into Kentucky was launched in 1778, and over one hundred braves and two hundred Canadians marched on Boonesboro. Boone was captured (again) and persuaded them they did not have enough men to capture the fort. He escaped in June and warned the fort. The main force, now numbering over four hundred, returned in September and encamped around the fort at Boonesboro. An attempt at peace failed, and a nine-day battle ensued. The Shawnee tried several ways to defeat Fort Boonesboro, including a fake retreat to draw out the settlers, tunneling under the walls and attempting to set fire to the fort. While this was going on, groups from the Native forces attacked area cabins and settlements. The Indians finally gave up and retreated.

The year 1779 saw more attacks of travelers along both the Wilderness and Limestone Roads. The Kentucky militia determined to counterattack and marched to a Shawnee village. Although they burned about forty cabins and stole 143 horses, they were forced to retreat, with the attacking Shawnee chasing them for about ten miles. Other attacks across the region continued throughout the year.

2

FOUNDING OF LEXINGTON

In 1774, when William McConnell made his first trip, his intent was to begin searching for land to claim. He returned in the spring of 1775 with his brother Francis and a party of five other men, mostly family. By May, the group had grown to a total of eleven men. They established a base camp on the north branch of the Elkhorn River and commenced making surveys in groups. When finished there, they moved to the middle fork of the Elkhorn, later to be named Town Branch when Lexington was established. Again, they made surveys, erected small huts or other "improvements" and planted corn, the key bases on which to make a claim to land under Virginia law. The planting of a corn crop was particularly important for two reasons: mature corn plants were generally taller than local vegetation, and corn was not native to Kentucky and thus positive evidence of an intent to settle. William and Francis McConnell each laid claim to a four-hundred-acre tract as well as a one-thousand-acre "preemption." Within William's tract were the "sinking springs" that today we know as McConnell's Spring.

That summer, the group was camped around McConnell's springs. While there, staking out land claims and ambitions no doubt growing, they began envisioning a new settlement in or near their lands. Various names were considered, including purportedly York and Lancaster, when word reached them from Fort Harrod of the encounter between the English troops and American minutemen at Lexington, Massachusetts. They decided to name their proposed settlement Lexington after the armed engagement (not the town, as is sometimes mistakenly assumed).

While the name was chosen, the site was not, or at least it is not clear that it was. The McConnell group may have considered the name for their encampment at the springs. Certainly, by the time the Virginia legislature in 1776 created Fayette County and named Lexington as its seat, there must have been some agreed-upon spot or building where the county commissioners were to meet; but the time was not ripe for a settlement. Indian raids were still a prospect. Perrin's *History* baldly states: "The summer of 1776 found no white man in all the length and breadth of the present Fayette County. McConnell's cabin was deserted and falling to pieces." The year 1777 saw a dramatic increase in the number of such raids, as the British encouraged the Indians to attack settlers as part of their war strategy. Many fled back east, and those remaining retreated to the few forts in the area: Fort Harrod, Fort Boonesboro and the fortified Logan's Station. William and Francis McConnell were among those who stayed in Fort Harrod.

At the end of March 1779, Ensign Robert Patterson, an officer in Captain Levi Todd's military company at Fort Harrod, was ordered to take men and establish a garrison at some point north of the Kentucky River, which is to say, within the present Fayette County. All of the then current forts and fortified settlements (called "stations") were south of the Kentucky River, and the desire, from a military standpoint, was to establish a "point of the spear" across the river to be the defense against future Indian attacks. Keeping or delaying the attacking force north of the river would give the forts below it more time to prepare.

Patterson had explored the area four years previously and remembered a particular spring. He led his company of twenty-five men through the forest to that site and camped about the first of April. There they began the work of felling trees, clearing a space of cane and other growth and erecting a plain blockhouse surrounded by a stockade fence overlooking the spring. The site was roughly in the middle of the present block on Main Street between South Broadway and South Mill Street. The spring, which ran in all seasons, flowed down to Town Branch.

Three things then combined to make this blockhouse stockade the beginning of the town of Lexington: the general defeat of the Indians in recent fights made the area safer (though not completely so), the blockhouse provided a central point of defense and a law of Virginia's granting extensive "settlement rights" to claimants in Kentucky was to expire in 1780. A number of cabins began to be erected around the blockhouse.

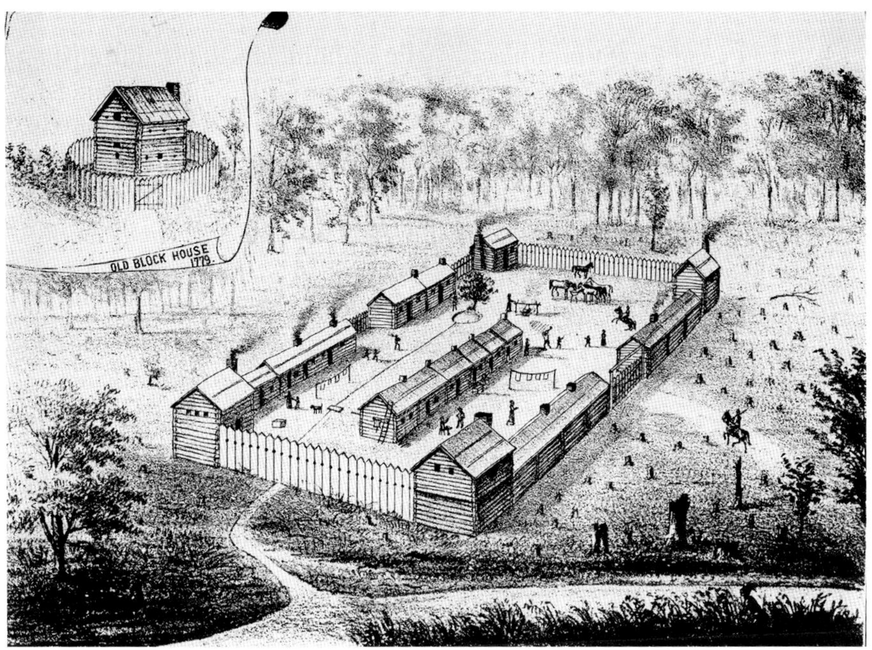

"Lexington Station" with Town Branch in the foreground. *Courtesy of the Bullock Photographic Collection, Transylvania University Library.*

To McConnell and his men, then, goes credit for the naming of Lexington; but to Patterson and his men goes the credit for the actual founding of a permanent settlement of that name.

What happened next is a source of some confusion. Some histories of Lexington speak of "Fort Lexington" as though there was only one such structure, but research has revealed that there were, in fact, two fortified structures. One can be characterized as a defensible community or station and the other as a military fort.

A station took several forms, but the key characteristic was a group of cabins or huts in a defensive array into which people and animals could retreat while relief was sought from a nearby fort. It could be modest like Daniel Boone's second station (after Fort Boonesboro), which he established in eastern Fayette County, near the current community of Athens. It consisted of several half-faced huts with slanted roofs sloping back to the ground which faced each other around a fire. Log fences connected the huts, making it more an enclosure for animals but with the ability to watch each direction. More fully developed stations, like Bryan's Station in northern present-day Fayette County, consisted of log cabins, again facing each other, with no outside windows and with log walls connecting the corners of the cabins.

The Lexington Station appears to have been an outgrowth from the original two-story log blockhouse erected by Patterson and his party. Perrin describes it as having "the shape of a parallelogram, two sides of which were framed by the exposed walls of two rows of cabins, the extreme ends of the fort being defended by stockades of sharpened posts." In the center of the enclosed space ran a single row of cabins, and there was sufficient room for both residents outside the fort and livestock in the event of a raid. Perrin goes on to describe the walls of the fort as running from the blockhouse across what would become Main Street to a cabin built by James Masterson, thence back across Main to another structure, then crossing the future Mill Street and back to the blockhouse. It appears the simple plan was to take existing cabins as corners and build walls and other cabins to fill in the boundaries. This fortified enclosure was completed in 1782. The ever-flowing spring, enclosed by the stockade, provided a source of fresh water. However, the location of the cabins and stockade was in a valley, overlooked by a high hill to the south and more slowly rising ground to the north. An attacking force could easily see, and fire, into the stockade.

At the same time, which may be the source of the confusion, another fort was being erected at the direction of Colonel John Todd in April 1781 at what is now the northwest corner of High and South Broadway. On April 15, 1781, Todd wrote the governor of Virginia to advise him the fort had been constructed and send him a bill for reimbursement of Todd's expenses. The fort is described in the *History of Pioneer Lexington* as an open square eighty feet on a side, with seven-foot-thick timber walls filled with packed dirt, nine feet tall on the outside, but narrowed to five feet tall on the inside, thus providing a shelf for men to stand on behind the upper portion of the walls when defending the fort. The corners of the fort extended in diamond-shaped points to allow defending fire along the exterior walls. A "moat" four to five feet deep surrounded the structure. In the center of the fort was a magazine building twenty by twenty feet. The magazine was the only building within the walls. Todd's sketch of the fort shows the entrance on the east with a road turning north and labeled "way to water," that is, down the hill toward Town Branch.

These are clearly two different structures, though both are called the "new fort" at various times in various writings. One was a place of quick refuge in the case of a raid; the other was designed to withstand light artillery fire. The placement of Todd's fort also made military sense. Its

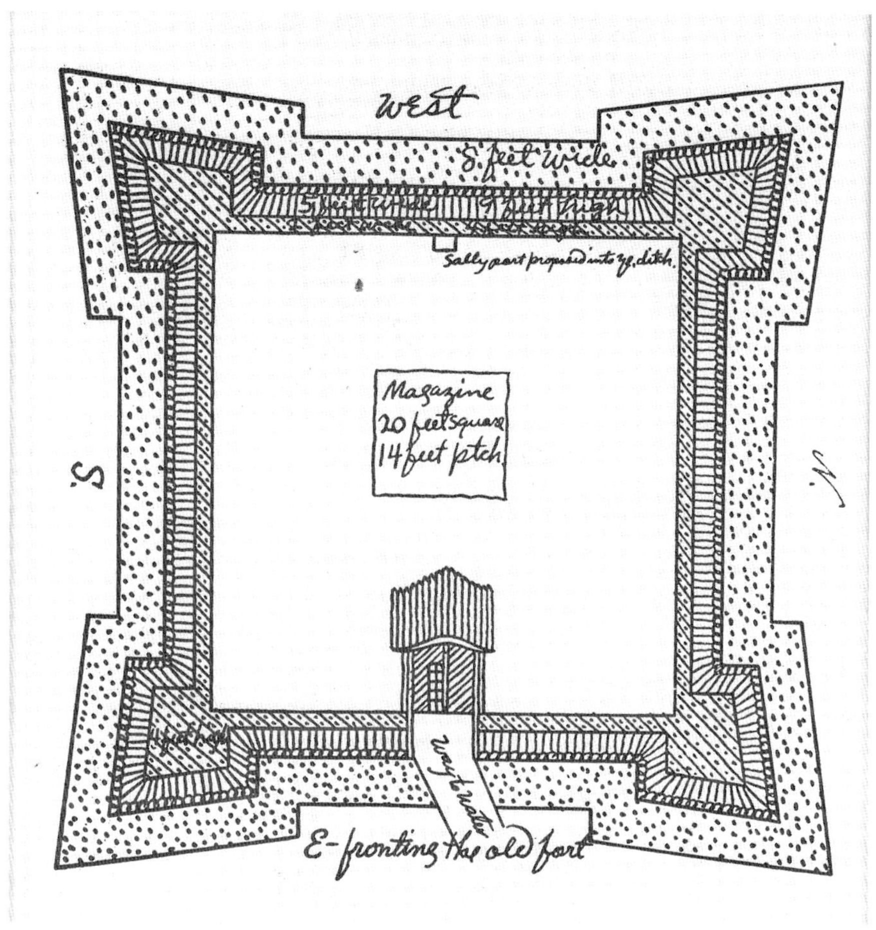

A drawing of Fort Lexington, erected at West High and South Broadway Streets. The note "way to water" indicates the direction downhill to Town Branch. *Public domain.*

location was near the top of a hill on the road to Fort Harrod, overlooking both the emerging community below at Town Branch and the approach from Fort Harrod. When the town of Lexington was platted into lots, the end of the town stopped across from the location of the fort. It would not be long before the walls of the lower blockade, perhaps in some confidence of protection from Todd's fort, were breached by the new Main Street. Todd's fort would be torn down in 1787, evidence that the need for a fortified defensive structure was gone.

It was time to formalize the creation of a town. On January 25, 1780, forty-seven settlers of Lexington signed the "Articles of Agreement between the Citizens of Lexington." Not unlike the famous Mayflower Compact, it set forth the basic understanding of the infant community on how it would be governed. Whether there was one author or many or it was based on some traditional format of common knowledge among the settlers is not known. This agreement called for the election of trustees, who met for the first time on March 26 in one of the log cabins in the downtown fort. Two primary resolutions were passed at this meeting.

The first was addressed to the Court of Fayette County, established in 1780 when Kentucky County was divided into three counties, but evidently without a regular place of meeting. The court was informed that "if they should deem Lexington a proper place for holding courts in the future, the sum of £30 in gold or silver, or the value thereof in Continental currency, will be granted by the Trustees for public buildings." The Virginia legislature having designated Lexington as the county seat, the town trustees now responded by inviting the court to reside there as well by offering to erect a courthouse.

FAYETTE COUNTY COURT HOUSE, LEXINGTON, KY.

Fayette County Courthouse, 1806. *Courtesy of the Lexington Public Library.*

Adam Rankin House, original portion built 1784, the oldest surviving house in Lexington. *Katrina Ockerman.*

The second resolution called for the town to be laid out with streets and two sizes of lots. The in-lots were to be one-third acre each and the out-lots five acres. Each free man over twenty-one years of age, each widow and each "young man" who was clearly independent would receive by lottery one in-lot or town lot and one out-lot, the intent being to cluster dwellings in the town and move livestock and other agricultural pursuits to the edges. No fewer than thirty of the in-lots, or about ten acres, were to be reserved for "public uses." The town lots ran along Town Branch. Out-lots to the south extended up the hill to near what is now Maxwell Street. In contrast, the out-lots to the north ran to north of Seventh Street. The eastern and western town boundaries were roughly Eastern Avenue and along a line 150 feet east of Jefferson Street, respectively. Each recipient of a lot was required to pay "a proportionable part of the money necessary to build the public houses and expenses arising toward good order and regularity in the town."

Provision was made for the platting of the lots, and the trustees, meeting the day after Christmas 1781, formally adopted the plan.

A further step toward formal township status had been taken earlier in the year. Daniel Boone, who had a cabin at Boone's Station, near present-day Athens in eastern Fayette County, was elected as the representative of Fayette County in the Virginia legislature. On June 21, Boone introduced

The Patterson Cabin on the campus of Transylvania University. *Katrina Ockerman.*

a bill in the legislature to formally create the town of Lexington. It took almost a year for the legislature to act, but on May 6, 1782, the act was passed and Lexington formally chartered. Over two years before, the residents of Lexington, under their own agreement and perhaps with little real lawful authority, had elected their own trustees. The Virginia act now officially named John Todd, Robert Patterson, William Mitchell, Andrew Steel, William Henderson, William M'Cownald (McConnell) and William Steel as the first trustees. The act also set aside 640 acres of unappropriated land, plus an additional 70 acres the town trustees had purchased, as the bounds of the new town, and empowered the trustees to convey deeds to the lots, settle disputes regarding same and make rules and orders regarding buildings. Together with other Virginia laws pertaining to towns, the act gave the trustees authority to organize and run the town of Lexington.

Robert Patterson, head of the military company that built the first blockhouse, built a log cabin around 1783 on one of the southwestern outlots, which in time came to be numbered as 331 Patterson Street. In 1901, this cabin was removed to a location in Ohio, then in 1939 returned and reconstructed on the campus of Transylvania University along Third Street near Gratz Park. This cabin is thought to be one of the earliest cabins built in Lexington and is the earliest surviving.

3

FROM SETTLEMENT TO VILLAGE

With the end of the Revolutionary War and the concomitant end of Indian raids, Lexington entered into a period of rapid growth in the mid-1780s, converting it from a frontier settlement to a rural village. The fertile and gently rolling land was attractive to immigrants to the area, and Lexington lay then, as it does now, at the axis of major routes of travel. The Wilderness Road from the Cumberland Gap led there, as did what was called the Buffalo Trace, or Limestone Road, from the river port of Limestone (now Maysville), where river traffic from Pittsburgh landed. Eventually, a road to Louisville led off to the west. It was virtually impossible to go through Kentucky in any direction without coming to or through Lexington.

Kentucky's first schoolhouse, and the first public building to be erected on the public square set out on the town plat, was built on what is now Tandy Park, on the west side of the current Old Courthouse, in 1783. Teacher John McKinney returned after lunch to the one-room log cabin that served as the school and was surprised by a wildcat hiding under his desk. The wildcat leaped on his back, digging in its claws, and the struggle began. McKinney's shouts attracted other people to the scene, thus providing witnesses to the story. The fight ended when McKinney killed the animal, either with his bare hands or by trapping it under the desk upended in the struggle. The witnesses helped him back to the stockade to dress his wounds.

The significance of this event is not that it was the first time a wildcat was associated with Lexington, nor that the local environment was such that a curious wild animal was comfortable invading a human settlement and even entering a cabin.

The significance is that the founders of the settlement, still yet a collection of cabins, valued education enough to take time from other demands to erect a schoolhouse dedicated to that purpose and persuade or perhaps even hire one of their more educated members to be the teacher, beginning the tradition of Lexington as a center of education, which continues today. It is also noteworthy that there were enough children in the settlement to even warrant a school.

After building the schoolhouse, the next public building was a courthouse, although it was not put on the public square. It was built on the northwest corner of Main and Main Cross (Broadway) in 1782. Previously, sessions of court were held in one of the cabins in the stockade. This first courthouse was a two-story log structure about thirty-six feet on a side, with two rooms on each floor and cellars below. What is described as a "crude log hut" was built next door as the jail.

Within only five years, the courthouse was deemed inadequate, and a committee appointed by the town trustees chose the public square as the location for the second courthouse, the place where successive courthouses would stand until the current Fayette County circuit and district courthouses were built along the east side of North Limestone.

This new courthouse was built of dressed limestone under the direction of Captain John Cape, who would later build a similar courthouse for Jefferson County. The new design was two stories tall, with four rooms and a central hall on each level, covered by a hip roof with a cupola. It is not reported which of the rooms served as the actual courtroom, though typically it would have been on the second floor.

Two years later, the old jail was also replaced with a stone building on the west side of Limestone Street, north of Short Street, twenty by thirty-two feet in size. Nearby were a whipping post and stocks for the temporary punishment of offenders. Lancaster notes these were used frequently to save the cost of boarding prisoners who would otherwise have been put in the jail. This jail would be replaced in 1797, after only seven years, further evidence of the growth of the community.

The former log courthouse was then sold, and by 1790 it was owned by John Bradford, who had begun publication of the *Kentucky Gazette*, the state's first newspaper, in 1787. He moved his printing press and office there. His residence was on the second floor, and the printing shop and a post office occupied the first.

The growing village needed more than courthouses and jails. It needed churches, merchants and a marketplace.

Although the town trustees made provisions for a site for a "house of public worship" near the public square—another example of what today would be called land-use planning—the first church was not erected there due to a provision of Virginia law. In contrast with other colonies, Virginia formally recognized the Church of England as a state-supported church, imposing property taxes to support its ministers. In furtherance of this policy, Virginia prohibited the erection of any church building inside a town boundary that was not affiliated with the Episcopal Church.

In 1784, Reverend Adam Rankin, a Presbyterian minister from Virginia, built a small church on what is now South Limestone, opposite the present Virginia Avenue, which was outside the city limits and thus in compliance with the law. It is reported to have been the first church of any denomination in Lexington. He built his residence on the north side of High Street, between Upper and Mill Streets, on one of the in-lots. This house was moved in 1971, out of the path of the construction of a bank building, to a lot on South Mill Street, where it is preserved today as the oldest surviving house in Lexington.

While credit for the first church goes to the Presbyterians, other denominations were not far behind. The Town Fork Baptist Church was organized in 1786, meeting out of town on today's Old Frankfort Pike. Methodists began meeting in a cabin at the southwest corner of what is today Short and Deweese Streets, on a part of out-lot 23, which they purchased in 1814 and erected a brick building. At the time, the Methodist Societies were part of the Church of England, so they were lawfully permitted to have a church, the first, inside the city limits.

Upon achieving statehood in 1792, Kentucky did not adopt the Virginia church laws, and denominations began moving into the city. German Lutherans built a frame church and schoolhouse on the south side of High Street in 1799. This building burned to the ground around 1815, and it appears the Lutherans blended into the Methodist Church, a not untypical pattern on the frontier, as the German seminaries were unable to produce ministers fast enough to supply the number of Germans migrating into Kentucky and other western areas of the United States. The Methodists, after an intermediate location, moved to the High Street property in 1840. There is no deed of record transferring the property from the German Lutherans to the Methodists, which supports the proposition of a merger of the congregations.

In 1790, the first Black church in Kentucky, the African Baptist Church, was established in Lexington. In 1791, the members of Rankin's Mt. Zion Presbyterian Church moved to North Mill and erected a frame church, changing the name to First Presbyterian. In 1796, regular sessions began in a small frame church by Reverend James Moore, marking the establishment of Christ Church Episcopal at Market and Church Streets.

General James Wilkinson, the Revolutionary War soldier, arrived in Lexington in 1784 and opened the first general store. Originally, his goods came from Philadelphia, brought overland to Pittsburgh and then carried by flatboat on the Ohio River to the town of Limestone (later Maysville), to be transported overland to his new store. Later, as commerce developed down the Mississippi River to New Orleans, Wilkinson extended his trading downriver. Wilkinson would later reenter Lexington's history as part of the alleged conspiracy of Aaron Burr to separate the western states, including Kentucky, to form a new nation allied with Spain. Other traveling merchants held temporary stores in the fronts of various cabins, open only so long as their stock of merchandise lasted, then closing for the season to return east for more goods.

In 1785, James Bray opened Lexington's first tavern, located on West Main Street, and the following year John Higbee opened the first inn at the corner of High and Limestone Streets.

The town trustees may have ambitiously laid out a great number of in- and out-lots, but in 1785 Lexington was said to have consisted of only three rows of log cabins. These may have been the two outer walls and one inside line of cabins from the downtown stockade. There was also a scattering of other cabins being built on the town lots. Earlier, the existing settlers had drawn for lots. In that year, however, the trustees sold the first in-lots to newcomers.

The first market house was begun in 1791. A two story, twenty-five-by-fifty-foot structure, it was open below and enclosed as a large hall above. Given that the hall above was supported by sixteen brick pillars, each three feet square and twelve feet tall, it suggests that there were seven bays below for farmers and tradesmen to set up stalls. The market house was completed in the spring of 1792, coinciding with the admission of Kentucky as a state on June 1. Lexington was designated as the first and provisional capital. The first meetings of the new state legislature were held in the upper hall of the market house. The hope, if not expectation, of the town was that it would become the permanent capital of the new state. However, a fierce debate and rivalry between Lexington and the emerging riverport town of

Louisville erupted over the question. A committee of the legislature was deputized to review proposals and make a recommendation. The matter was settled when the town of Frankfort offered more land and building materials to win the honor.

As was the pattern with other public buildings, this market house was outgrown, and in 1795 the town trustees authorized construction of a new market house on the public square. Again two stories but this time of stone, it was surrounded by a post-and-rail fence twelve feet from the walls with gates at either end, either to hold livestock brought for sale or trade or to keep that livestock out of the market. A brick addition in 1803 extended the building to Short Street. This portion of the public square came to be called Cheapside, after the famous market area in London, England. A new street leading north to Third Street, taking parts of out-lots E and F, would be called Market Street.

According to Lancaster, tax records for 1795 revealed that Lexington had grown considerably from its original enclosed cabin stockade. There were twenty-six stores in addition to the traders operating out of the market house and nine "ordinaries"—a combination tavern and eating house—plus inns and boardinghouses. Businesses listed by Lancaster included hemp, baggage and rope factories or "walks"; a brewery and distillery; brickyards; tanning yards; a nail plant (evidence that frame buildings were succeeding logs); wheel, cabinet and furniture makers; a variety of "smiths"—blacksmith, whitesmith, coppersmith, locksmith, clocksmith, silver and goldsmiths—as well as a hatter, glover and saddler; shoe and boot makers; a weaver, dressmakers and tailors; and, in what was to become the "Horse Capital of the World," the first livery stable.

Town improvements during this period included removing tree stumps from Main Street and other primary streets, as well as the removal of livestock pens from the town center. The town trustees also authorized the construction of several bridges over Town Branch to facilitate access to and from the south end of town. At this time, the land on either side of Town Branch was designated as the Commons and the street flanking it to the north as Water Street. By 1795, the town was estimated to comprise some three to four hundred houses in addition to the commercial and public buildings, only fourteen years after the first town plat was approved.

4

HENRY CLAY COMES TO TOWN

Henry Clay arrived in Lexington from Virginia in 1797, having been admitted to the practice of law in that state. The following year, he was admitted to the practice of law in Kentucky by the court at Lexington. It was a fertile period for litigation in Fayette County. The haphazard methods of early surveys and staked claims produced a wealth of lawsuits over titles to land. It was a good place to start a law practice.

At the time, according to the records of the town trustees, Lexington had a population of "males above 12 years 462; Females above 12 years, 307; whites under 12 years, 346; Negroes 360." Fayette County as a whole, including the town, had a population of 2,247.

In later years, Clay liked to say he arrived in Lexington penniless and friendless, but that was more a campaign story than reality.

When Henry's father, a Baptist minister, died in 1781, he left him two slaves. An uncle left Clay a third. His mother inherited 464 acres of Virginia land. When Clay was fifteen, his stepfather sponsored him into a job with the local court, which in turn led to his being hired as secretary to George Wythe, the most respected and learned jurist of the state. Clay studied under Wythe for four years before Wythe arranged for him to take a job in the state attorney general's office, where he continued his studies another year. Clay was admitted to the Virginia bar at the age of twenty and left for Kentucky.

During this period, his mother and stepfather moved to Versailles, where his stepfather accumulated almost one thousand acres of land and several slaves and was a justice of the peace. Henry's older brother, John, was a Lexington merchant and was soon joined by another brother.

As important as his real family, however, was the extended family of attorneys who had studied under Wythe: John Breckinridge, George Nicholas and James Brown all had established practices in Lexington and began to refer cases to Clay. In time, he would substantially take over their practices and clients when they left Lexington for other places.

Henry Clay, circa 1805, the earliest known image of the statesman. *Courtesy of Ashland, the Henry Clay Estate.*

Within two years, Clay married a daughter of Colonel Thomas Hart, a co-founder of the Transylvania Company, which financed early settlers in Kentucky. Hart owned thousands of acres of land and had substantial business interests. Clay and his new wife bought a house on North Mill Street from Colonel Hart, who lived next door, and Clay established his law office across the street. He began doing legal work for his father-in-law. Clay's personal success was not entirely due to his connections; he brought a fine legal mind and a talent as a speaker to the job. In only seven years, according to tax rolls, he owned more than six thousand acres of land (some accepted as legal fees), including several town lots, slaves and horses.

Lexington experienced similar growth as a town. The early educational effort of a schoolhouse had expanded to a number of private schools.

In 1780, the Virginia legislature chartered the Transylvania Seminary as a public school. It opened its doors in 1785, conducting classes in a log house near Danville. Nine years later, attracted by the offer of an entire out-lot, the school relocated to Lexington and in 1783 erected a two-story brick building on what it called the College Square, the present Gratz Park.

Almost immediately, however, it had competition. In 1790, the Kentucky legislature chartered the Kentucky Academy, which started classes in Woodford County, near Pisgah, in 1796. There was intense competition between the institutions located so near each other. The problem was resolved by act of the General Assembly in 1798 when the merger of the two schools was approved. The new institution became known as Transylvania University at that time and continued in Lexington, awarding its first bachelor of arts degree in 1802, the first west of the mountains.

Henry Clay's law office. *Katrina Ockerman.*

Henry Clay became a professor of law and politics at the University in 1805 and later served on its board of trustees for a total of eighteen years. Throughout his public career, Clay promoted the university and assisted in recruiting faculty. Indeed, for the next several decades, it is difficult to separate Lexington and Clay, as his life continually intersected with that of the town.

In 1803, Clay was elected to the General Assembly, representing Fayette County. He introduced legislation to move the capital back to Lexington, which did not pass.

In 1802, the Kentucky Insurance Company was chartered by the legislature. Clay and his father-in-law were stockholders, and Colonel Hart had a seat on the board of directors. Ostensibly formed to insure goods shipped downriver to New Orleans for sale, the charter gave the company authority to issue bank notes, effectively giving it banking powers and a monopoly as the only state bank. A faction in the General Assembly attempted to revoke the charter. The measure passed, only to be vetoed by the governor. Clay successfully marshaled the votes to sustain the veto.

In 1803, the first commercial stagecoach began operating in Lexington, leaving twice weekly from the Kentucky Hotel and running, via Winchester, to Olympian Springs, a mineral springs spa resort in southern Bath County.

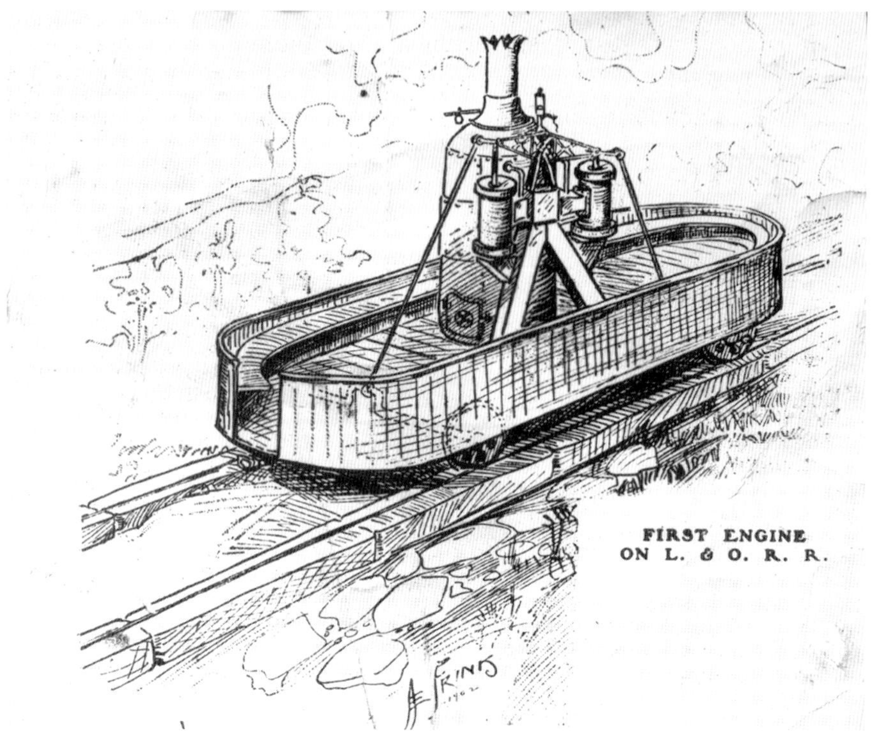

The first railroad engine on the Lexington & Ohio Railroad. *Courtesy of the University of Kentucky Archives.*

Clay owned an interest in the hotel, and his father-in-law owned the resort. They likely owned all or a large share of the stagecoach company.

During this period, Lexington took on more of the aspects of a sophisticated village. Brick sidewalks were laid in the business section of town, and seven bridges crossed Town Branch, which by the turn of the century had been straightened and walled with rock to form what was called a canal, although it was not deep enough for commercial traffic. By 1809, the town trustees had passed an ordinance prohibiting wheeled carriages from driving on the sidewalks, indicating that the sidewalks were in better condition than the streets. Later, the trustees purchased crushed stone to be placed on the principal streets.

The year 1806 saw the erection of Fayette County's third courthouse, on the site of the prior stone building, which had been demolished. The new judicial building was three stories tall, with a clock tower, belfry and tall spire topped by a weathervane at a cost of $15,000. Small two-story outbuildings on either side contained offices for the sheriff, county surveyor and circuit and county clerks. Henry Clay was openly critical of the design, calling it a "miserable building," perhaps more a lawyer's criticism of the interior's use and functionality than architectural commentary.

Former vice president Aaron Burr was traveling in the western states in 1806, meeting with various officials and supporters. In the fall of that year, the newspaper in Frankfort began a series of stories, in reality politically partisan articles, alleging that Burr was in the state conspiring to separate Kentucky from the United States and join it into a new country along the Mississippi River allied with Spain. General James Wilkinson, the former Lexington merchant now returned to military service, was said to be among the conspirators. The full history of the Spanish Conspiracy is well beyond the scope of this history, including Burr's trial for treason a year later in Virginia, but the allegations were a lively topic of conversation in Lexington. In the fall of 1806, the U.S. Attorney James Hamilton Daveiss asked the federal judge in Frankfort for an order arresting Burr on charges of attempting to incite war with Mexico and sever the union. Burr retained Henry Clay as chief defense counsel.

A period of legal maneuvering ensued, and the trial was postponed more than once due to the absence of witnesses for the prosecution. Finally, Clay was successful in obtaining dismissal of the charges against Burr.

The first Jockey Club was formed in 1797 at a meeting at Postlethwait's Tavern, four years after the town trustees banned racing on city streets and confined the matches to the Commons along Town Branch. A racetrack was laid out on a portion of what is now the Lexington Cemetery and adjoining land. It was called the Williams Brothers Race Track after the owners of the land. The Jockey Club held regular meets there for twelve years. In 1809, the club was reorganized into the Lexington Jockey Club, which took charge of the track.

The town had been governed by seven trustees, elected each year in nonpartisan elections, since its official creation by the Virginia legislature. In 1810, the citizens believed the number of trustees, the police and town funds were inadequate and petitioned the Kentucky legislature for a law allowing them to make changes. The result was the number of trustees was enlarged to eleven, a poll or voting tax established and a twenty-five-cent tax per one hundred dollars of value assessed on real and personal property.

Lexington's commercial activity continued to grow. The *Gazette* reported in 1811 that, among the larger enterprises in the town, there were 9 tanneries, 139 distilleries, 5 gunpowder mills, 1 paper mill, 13 rope walks, 2 cut nail

Left: Benjamin Gratz, by Thomas Sully, 1831. *Courtesy of the Rosenbach Museum & Library, Philadelphia, Pennsylvania.*

Right: Maria Gratz, by Thomas Sully, 1831. *Courtesy of the Rosenbach Museum & Library, Philadelphia, Pennsylvania.*

factories, 4 hat factories and 6 cotton and wool spinning mills, in addition to the many individuals pursuing solo or small businesses.

Outside of the courthouse, the Market House was the most important public building, and laws were passed to regulate its affairs. The office of Clerk of the Market was established, and among his duties was keeping the official set of weights and measures against which those of every merchant were compared three times a year, which he would mark as inspected and receive a fee. If anyone used an unmarked weight or measure, the clerk could seize the articles and impose a fine. More prosaically, it was also his duty to see the market was swept clean twice a week and to seize and burn "unwholesome provisions" offered for sale.

At the start of the nineteenth century, there were only five medical schools in the United States, one of which and the only one in the West was at Transylvania University. After it was reorganized in 1815, it began to grow in prominence and students. By 1818, however, three faculty members had become at odds with one another. Dr. Benjamin Dudley attempted to have Dr. William Richardson fired but was blocked by Dr. Daniel Drake. Drake then publicly criticized Dudley's performance of a coroner's autopsy.

Each published insulting comments about the other and resulted in Dudley challenging Drake to a duel. Drake disagreed with the practice and declined, but Richardson accepted in his place. Dudley severely wounded Richardson in the exchange and then, true to his profession, saved the man's life. The medical school was recognized as one of the best in the nation in the first half of the century, but by 1859 it had closed.

The more than five thousand residents of Lexington received the news of another war with Great Britain, the War of 1812, with enthusiasm. Clay, now in Congress, belonged to the group of congressmen called the Young Hawks for advocating the conflict. Six companies of men responded to the call for volunteers in Lexington alone, and several prominent citizens became officers. Kentucky as a whole contributed more than four thousand troops, almost all of whom fought in the Northwest Territory against the Indians and British there. Most of the gunpowder used by the American forces was manufactured at the Trotter Powder Mill on the Frankfort Pike in Lexington.

This period saw the arrival of two famous and one to-become-famous individuals.

President James Monroe visited Lexington on July 2, 1819, and stayed for five days. This was the first visit by a sitting president. He gave an address at Transylvania University.

Jefferson Davis, one day to become the only president of the Confederate States, arrived in 1821. He spent the next two years as a student at Transylvania before transferring to West Point. While in Lexington, he roomed at the house of the postmaster, Joseph Ficklin, at the southwest corner of High and Limestone Streets. Among the friends Davis made in Lexington was Henry Clay Jr., who would also join him as a cadet at West Point. Davis and the younger Clay later served together at the Battle of Buena Vista (where Henry Clay Jr. was killed) during the war with Mexico, and Davis would later serve in the U.S. Senate with Henry Clay.

On May 15, 1825, the Marquis de Lafayette, on a tour though the United States, which he had helped achieve independence, arrived for a brief one-day stay at the home of Major John Keene on the Versailles Road, having come from Louisville. The Keene House is now part of the Keeneland Race Course property.

While Lexington was improving its streets, the same could not be said for the roads through the state on which Lexington's development as a commercial center depended. As early as 1817, the first turnpike company was chartered. The Lexington & Louisville Turnpike Road Company was formed as a private company to improve the road between the two towns, with stockholders living in Versailles, Middletown and Shelbyville as well as the two cities. The Maysville & Lexington Company was chartered the following year. Neither company, however, did much work for several years. By the late 1820s and certainly by the early 1830s, a serious program of construction of graded and macadamized or paved roads was underway. Perrin's *History* reports that the Maysville road, known locally as the Paris Pike, cost $426,400 to complete, including construction of thirteen toll houses and six covered bridges.

A turnpike was a toll road. The name comes from a pike, or long pole, stretched across a road to block passage until the required fee was paid, at which time the pole was either raised or turned out of the way. Tollbooths were typically set every five miles, and differing rates applied to different users of the road. A single rider might pay five cents, herds of cattle were charged by the head, less for herds of sheep or hogs, up to as much as thirty-five cents for a stagecoach. The resulting roads were called "pikes," and the prevalence of these privately developed roads around Lexington is shown by the frequent use of that word in a name: Old Frankfort Pike, Tates Creek Pike and so on. Almost every major road leading from Lexington was at one time a turnpike, although modern nomenclature favors changing the name from pike to road. A map shows the lands of the Henry Clay family with the location of "toll houses" along his fences on both Tates Creek Pike and Richmond Pike.

Individuals, cities, counties and even the state bought stock in these companies to provide the funds for the initial improvements. The irony, in the case of governmental investment, was that a citizen would pay taxes, from which funds purchases of stock in toll road companies were made, which in turn charged the citizen a toll for the privilege of traveling over the road.

The state established a Bureau of Internal Improvements to regulate tolls and state participation, but it was abolished in the 1850s. After that time, until the twentieth century, the state had no role in highway development and maintenance. In the 1840s, there were almost nine hundred miles of toll roads in Kentucky, and by the Civil War virtually every road outside of a town was privately owned.

In 1811, Congress began construction of the National Road, beginning at Cumberland, Maryland, with the ultimate intent of extending it through Ohio, Illinois and Indiana as far as St. Louis, Missouri. By 1818, this first national roadway had reached the Ohio River at Wheeling, Virginia (now West Virginia), which greatly enhanced the transportation of goods, livestock and people to Lexington via the river and Maysville, as well as to

Toll gate building spanning Harrodsburg Road, 1895. *Courtesy of the Barton K. Battaile Collection.*

Louisville. Work was underway to take the National Road the next extension to Zanesville, Ohio, in the late 1820s when Kentucky, which the road was bypassing, sought to procure a branch from Zanesville south through Maysville to Lexington, thence through Tennessee and other states to New Orleans, Lexington's traditional object of export. The General Assembly adopted a resolution in 1828 instructing its U.S. senators (which it could "instruct," since it elected them at that time) and requesting its representatives to attempt to pass the appropriate legislation. The House passed legislation for this purpose in the spring of that year, but it failed in the Senate.

The road got as far as Vandalia, Illinois, before funding ran out in 1838, and in 1840, Congress voted to end the project and turn the sections of the road over to the states, where most become toll roads. Henry Clay cast the deciding vote to stop federal involvement.

By the 1830s, Louisville was growing faster than Lexington and exceeding it in size, due largely to the river traffic, which had to stop there to portage around the Falls of the Ohio River at Louisville. So long as river traffic with New Orleans consisted mostly of flatbed boats floating downstream to that city, where it was customary to break up the boats and sell the lumber before returning on foot or by horse to Kentucky, Lexington could compete. With the advent of the steamboat in the 1830s, however, traffic could now power upstream to Louisville and between Louisville and Cincinnati and Philadelphia. It is interesting to speculate whether, had a branch of the National Road extended through Lexington as the General Assembly desired, more commercial traffic would have been diverted from the river to an improved overland route to New Orleans with the consequence that Lexington would never have lost ground to Louisville. As it was, Louisville was put on the path of growth and development at the expense of Lexington. By the 1820s, Lexington was in what has been described as a state of stunted growth from which it would not really recover until the arrival of the interstates in the 1970s.

One of the most dramatic, and tragic, events in Lexington's history occurred in 1833. The first suggestion of trouble came the year before, the same year Lexington was formally chartered as a town and its government changed from the trustee form to mayor and council. The first mayor was Charlton Hunt, and a four-man city council was elected from each of four wards. In that year, there was a small cholera outbreak, but the faculty at the Transylvania University medical school reassured the population there was nothing to fear. At the time, the connection between a lack of sanitary conditions and the disease had not been established.

The old town trustees had the power to select their own successors and fill vacancies. Now, the first popular elections were held, a workhouse was established and life appeared to be normal. In May, Robert S. Todd, father of then fourteen-year-old Mary, the future wife of Abraham Lincoln, purchased a fourteen-room house on West Main Street, now preserved as a historic site. President Andrew Jackson, candidate for reelection, visited on September 29, 1832, and was guest of honor at a large barbecue given at the city limits on Winchester Road. He left the next day after attending services at First Presbyterian Church. And on New Year's Eve, the Episcopal Church took deed to a four-acre tract on East Third Street for a new cemetery.

5

EPIDEMIC AND RECESSION

In late May 1833, a major epidemic began and lasted until the next winter. The many springs and small streams running into Town Branch, a blessing of abundant fresh water in the founding days, became a liability as sewage flowing into the runoff proved to be a breeding ground for bacteria. The first week was described as "destructive"—deaths happened daily. Many, those who could, fled the town, and Lexington was almost emptied of residents. Businesses closed, and there was so little traffic or workers that grass began to grow in the city streets.

Those who were left had to cope with illness and death both in their households and in the streets, some turning their houses into makeshift hospitals. One survivor, a military officer, wrote just a few days into the crisis: "I would incomparably prefer a seven month's campaign in a furious war, than to under go [*sic*] another seven days such as these." In that short period, he said, "The Physicians are nearly worn out, nurses cannot be had, the coffin-makers are almost broken down, and the disease is still spreading." One of the coffin makers was Joseph Milward, who had opened a cabinet and furniture store in 1825, a business that continues today as Milward Funeral Directors. At the peak, 50 to 60 people died each day and over 1,500 others were stricken but survived. By the time the epidemic ended in August, 502 residents had died, about one-twelfth of the estimated population of 6,000.

Among those who stayed to help bury the dead were William "King" Solomon and U.S. Army cadet Jefferson Davis, the former Transylvania student and future Confederate president. Davis, a recent West Point

Police station, 1835. The tower was used to watch for fires. *Courtesy of the Barton K. Battaile Collection.*

graduate, and his troop were there on official duty on a recruiting trip. Solomon, however, was a town vagrant said to be immune from the disease because he never drank water, preferring whiskey.

The epidemic cast a pall over the economy of Lexington, and many were reluctant to invest in or move to the city, leading to a dramatic fall in land prices. Many others simply left. At the same time, there was a dramatic increase in the number of slaves sold at public auction to settle the estates of those who had died, become bankrupt or underwent foreclosure. Enslaved persons were, under Kentucky law at the time, a kind of property and, like any other asset, subject to sale to satisfy the claims of creditors. Lexington's reputation as a major slave selling center dates from this time.

There were, however, at least three positive outcomes from the plague. Church attendance, not surprisingly, increased. During the fall of 1833 and the following winter, revivals or "extraordinary meetings," depending on the denomination, were held and membership swelled.

The first city school was established in 1834, primarily to educate the orphans of the epidemic. And in 1833, the Lexington Orphan Asylum was established to care for those children. Before the disease had even run its course, in July, a meeting of citizens was called at the courthouse and $4,400 raised by public subscription. The funds were used to purchase a house and grounds on West Third Street, the present Hampton Court, and a board composed entirely of women was formed to administer the orphanage. Eventually incorporated as the Orphans Society of Lexington Inc., it continues today and is the oldest continually operating charity in Kentucky. In all that time, its board has been exclusively women.

What does not appear to have resulted from the summer of sickness was any organized civic program to address the source of the problem.

Lexington continued to develop, despite the epidemic, although land prices were severely depressed for a period. The Bank of Kentucky was established in the town in 1834; "Old Morrison" chapel building—construction had been interrupted—was completed; and St. Catherine's Academy, a Catholic girls' school, moved to Lexington from Scott County and would eventually evolve into the Lexington Catholic high school. In 1835, the first train between Frankfort and Lexington began runs, at the speed of about two and a half hours each way. The president of the railroad company was Robert Todd, the father of Mary Todd. The track ran across the rear of the Todd house land along Town Branch as it entered Lexington. In the same year, the Northern Bank of Kentucky opened with its headquarters in Lexington and branches in Paris, Barbourville and Covington. Edward P. Johnson & Co., with offices in the Phoenix Hotel, ran lines to Louisville, Cincinnati, Maysville, Ohio and Tennessee and even had a contract to carry U.S. Mail from Maysville to Florence, Alabama.

Just as Lexington was recovering from the cholera epidemic and its effects, the so-called Panic of 1837 struck the nation. A speculative bubble burst on the financial scene and began a five-year depression. Of some 850 banks in the nation, almost half failed in whole or part, the vast majority of those closing for good, and unemployment ran at record levels. Although mainly agricultural areas like Lexington and central Kentucky did not feel the effects as badly as the eastern cities, the depression is generally considered to have lasted five years.

Lexington, in fact, may have recovered earlier as, beginning in 1840, there was a series of major construction projects. On July 3, 1840, the cornerstone was laid for the second Masonic Grand Lodge Hall at Walnut and Short Streets. In 1840, the Methodists erected a new, large sanctuary on High, then called Hill Street. That church is still there, although parishioners worship in a newer sanctuary built in 1907 to replace the 1840 building. In 1842, the Main Street Christian Church building, two stories tall with a tower and seating eight hundred persons, was completed. After a schism in the congregation in 1870, both sides moved out. The building later served as a theater and a place for public gatherings until it was razed in 1903. The Lexington Theater, one of the largest in the West, opened on Short Street in 1844, and in that same year the fifth Market House was opened. It was of frame construction on the site of the prior market house, between Limestone and Upper, Vine and Water Streets. Basically a long shed where wagons were backed into stalls, it served until the sixth market house, Jackson Hall, was erected in 1879. The Second Presbyterian Church was built on Market Street and dedicated on October 31, 1847, replacing an 1815 structure. Just months before, the cornerstone of the new Christ Episcopal Church was laid, and the church was completed in 1848, likewise replacing an earlier (1814) building on the same site.

The Lexington Cemetery was organized in 1848 and acquired forty acres of land on West Main Street at the edge of town, including almost all of the former Williams Brothers racetrack. It opened the next year, just in time for another, though not as major, cholera outbreak when another 345 persons fell to the disease.

The first telegraph line was connected between Lexington and Louisville and the first message transmitted on March 6, 1848. Another tie between the two cities was made in 1852 when the Lexington & Frankfort and Louisville & Frankfort railroads were connected. Construction of a new bridge and the digging of a tunnel made it possible. No doubt as a result of increased traffic, the Lexington & Frankfort company built a new freight depot on West Vine near Patterson Street in 1854. The same year, David Sayre established the Transylvania Female Seminary. In 1855, the renamed Sayre Female Institute

Jackson Hall, facing Limestone Street along (old) Vine Street. The city market was on the first floor and city offices on the second. *Courtesy of the Barton K. Battaile Collection.*

relocated to a mansion on North Limestone opposite Second Street. A new First Baptist Church was begun in 1853 and finished in 1855, only to be destroyed by a fire that started in a livery across the street in 1859.

The 1850s also saw the purchase and development of what is now the central campus of the University of Kentucky for fairgrounds. The Maxwell Springs Company purchased twenty-five acres, including the spring of that name, and erected a grandstand and speaker's platform and several other buildings. This was the favored location for community celebrations and the drilling of its home militia. At the same time, the Kentucky Agricultural & Mechanical Association was formed and purchased land just south of Maxwell Springs as a site to hold annual fairs and exhibitions, including livestock and Thoroughbred horse shows.

In all, the two companies owned thirty-five acres south of Winslow Street (now Euclid Avenue) and west of Van Pelt (Rose) Street. The main amphitheater was 810 feet in circumference, and there were stables for 150 horses on the grounds. During the Civil War, the area was a military encampment for Union soldiers, who may have contributed to the destruction by fire of the amphitheater, a brick floral hall and other buildings in 1861. After the war, James Milligan purchased thirteen acres of this property and built the house known as Maxwell Place, now the residence of the president of the university. Future fairs would be held on the north side of Lexington, near the present Fifth and Race Streets, where the Kentucky Association had its racetrack.

While new structures were rising in Lexington, so were tensions over the practice of slavery.

The Kentucky Colonization Society had its office in Lexington. The society had as its aim the elimination of slavery by the gradual exportation of enslaved persons to Liberia on the west coast of Africa. It was most active in the 1840s and 1850s. Despite the fact that Clay viewed this process as the most logical solution, the society only relocated 658 people during its existence, which, of course, ended with the Civil War.

In 1845, the first issue of the *True American*, Cassius M. Clay's abolitionist newspaper, was published in Lexington from 6 North Mill Street. Cassius

Kentucky Association Race Track. *Courtesy of the Barton K. Battaile Collection.*

Clay, a cousin of Henry Clay, had been an open advocate for the end of slavery for several years. In August 1843, during a political rally north of Lexington, Cassius Clay challenged a statement made by a speaker and was struck by another man on the stage. A fight ensued, and in the scuffle Clay was shot. As the newspaper reported it: "In the affray, Mr. Clay was shot by Mr. Brown, the ball striking him just under the last rib on the left side, but coming in contact with the scabbard of Mr. Clay's bowie knife, do [*sic*] no injury. Mr. Brown was badly cut in several places about the head and face by Mr. Clay with the knife." Clay was brought under criminal indictment for his part but, defended by his cousin Henry, cleared of the charges.

In 1844, the Methodist Church in America, divided in principle over the question of whether bishops could enslave people, divided in fact into two denominations. The churches in the northern states reorganized as the Methodist Episcopal Church, those in the south as the Methodist Episcopal Church, South. Churches in border states were given the option to choose, and the Methodist Church in Lexington affiliated with the southern denomination. Today, a brass plaque over the central door into its sanctuary proclaims it is the "First Methodist Episcopal Church, South," despite the fact the two branches reunited in 1939. There would not be a branch of the northern Methodist denomination in Lexington until after the Civil War.

No history of Lexington would be complete without Mary Todd, and by extension Abraham Lincoln, although she actually spent almost none of her adult life in the community.

Mary Todd, born in Lexington on December 13, 1818, moved with her father and siblings in 1832 into what is now called the Mary Todd Lincoln House on West Main at the age of fourteen. Her father, Robert Todd, was a successful banker, and Mary was raised in luxury. Her mother died when Mary was six. Her father remarried in 1826, and Mary is said to have had a difficult relationship with her stepmother. The family of Todd's second wife owned a farm in Franklin County to which the family fled during the various cholera outbreaks. Although nominally living in Lexington for the next seven years, Mary, in fact, spent the last four away at a finishing school for young girls, learning the social graces as well as the French language. This time away from home could be ascribed variously to what a wealthy young girl did, to an escape from cholera or, according to some, to escape from her stepmother.

While Mary was away, her sister Elizabeth met and married Ninian W. Edwards, a Transylvania University graduate and son of a former governor of Illinois. The Edwardses settled in Springfield, Illinois, and in 1839 Mary

Mary Todd Lincoln. *Public domain.*

moved from Lexington to live with her sister and her husband. There she was very popular and courted by, among others, rising lawyer and politician Stephen A. Douglass, whom Lincoln would famously debate.

It was Abraham Lincoln, however, who won her heart, and they married in 1842, thus creating a personal connection to Lexington for the future president. He already had a political connection.

Henry Clay was Lincoln's ideal statesman and politician. Lincoln first voted for Clay for president in 1832, and in 1844 he actively campaigned for Clay, inviting Clay, on behalf of the Springfield Clay Club, to make an address there during the race. In the famous Lincoln-Douglas debates with his wife's former suitor, Lincoln quoted Clay over forty times. As Lincoln later prepared his first inaugural address, an edition of Clay's speeches was among only four books the president-elect consulted.

Did the personal and political connections ever lead to a meeting between Clay and Lincoln? That topic is hotly debated and has no definite answer. Robert Todd and Clay were contemporaries and, as active businessmen as well as wealthy men in the community, the two knew each other more than just socially. Clay is reported to have told the young Mary Todd that she would be among the first he would invite to the White House if he were elected president.

Mary and Abraham Lincoln visited Lexington several times prior to his election as president, staying often at the Todd house on Main Street. Lincoln represented his father-in-law on occasion in legal matters in Lexington and probated his estate. When Lincoln was elected to the U.S. House of Representatives in 1847, he and Mary stayed in Lexington for a month on his way to Washington, D.C. Lincoln was in the audience when Clay delivered a speech in the Market House on November 13, 1847. To these instances of proximity, a recent acquisition by the Henry Clay Memorial Foundation is a book of speeches of Clay's inscribed, "To Abraham Lincoln: With constant regard to friendship H. Clay Ashland 11 May 1847." How and why it was given is not yet known. Its date precedes the date of Clay's speech by just a few months.

It is hard to imagine that Lincoln, married into a family that socialized with Clay and counted him a personal friend, with cause to visit Lexington frequently and idolizing Clay, would not have made a great effort to arrange a meeting, either at Ashland or the Todds' house or at some social or political event. Proof of such a meeting, however, remains undiscovered.

6
THE DEATH OF CLAY

Henry Clay lost his final bid for the presidency in 1848 after failing to win the Whig Party's nomination for office. He retired to Lexington intending to remain at his farm, Ashland. However, he was prevailed upon to serve one more term in the U.S. Senate in 1849 and returned to Congress to fashion what became known as the Compromise of 1850, even though his health was suffering. On June 29, 1852, Clay died at the age of seventy-five. He was the first person to lie in state in the rotunda of the national Capitol. His body was returned to Ashland for a night, followed by a memorial service on its lawn the following morning. Then his funeral cortege left Ashland to travel through Lexington on the way to the cemetery. Although Lexington's population at the time was about 9,000, it is said over 100,000 people gathered to pay their respects. All businesses were closed, many of the buildings were draped in black and the crowd watched in silent respect as his coffin passed through town.

If one man had the potential to succeed Henry Clay as Lexington's dominant political figure, if not one of the nation's, it was John C. Breckinridge. His political career began to rise as Clay's waned. Where Clay was the youngest Speaker of the House of Representatives, Breckinridge was, and still is, the youngest Vice President of the United States. Vice President Dan Quayle, seemingly very young when elected at age forty-seven in 1989 with President George H.W. Bush, was eleven years older than Breckinridge was at his election. Breckinridge, in fact, barely met the minimum age requirement for election, being thirty-six when he took office.

Henry Clay's funeral procession. *Courtesy of the Barton K. Battaile Collection.*

Breckinridge was born near Lexington in 1821 to a long-established and politically active family. It was the resignation of his grandfather John Breckinridge from the U.S. Senate to become attorney general in 1806 that occasioned the first election of Henry Clay to serve the balance of his term.

Breckinridge graduated from Centre College in Danville, attended Princeton University and then studied law at Transylvania University. In 1840, he was admitted to the bar and began his law practice in Lexington. Nine years later, at the age of twenty-nine, he was elected to the Kentucky House of Representatives, and then, in 1851, he was elected to Congress representing Lexington. Although not in office for the crucial votes on Clay's Compromise of 1850, Breckinridge's first term overlapped with the final two years of Clay's service in the Senate.

Breckinridge was reelected in 1853 and served the two-year term, choosing not to run again in 1855. In that year, he declined President Franklin Pierce's nomination to become ambassador to Spain, which would have taken him out of the country. Instead, he sought the nomination for vice president and, running with James Buchanan, was elected to that office in 1856 at the age of thirty-five.

Henry Clay's statue in the Lexington Cemetery. *Katrina Ockerman.*

Having been the new president's running mate, however, did not mean he had much influence on the administration. In fact, Breckinridge had opposed Buchanan at the party convention and was largely ignored by the president while in office. However, as Buchanan's administration fell in popular support, Breckinridge's prestige rose.

By November 1859, he was back in Lexington awaiting the results of the vote by the Kentucky legislature on his bid for election to the U.S. Senate. He won that contest handily and returned to Washington, D.C., as vice president, senator-elect and candidate for the presidency. In 1860, he was the nominee of the Southern Democrats in a four-way race for the White House, coming in second in electoral votes to Lincoln. Expelled from the Senate, along with some other senators, for his support of the southern states, Breckinridge became a general and then secretary of war for the Confederacy. After the surrender of Lee, and fearing a potential trial for treason, he fled through Florida first to Cuba, then to exile in England and Canada. After a grant of amnesty in 1869, he returned to Lexington to practice law but never ran for office again. He died in Lexington in 1875.

The town Breckinridge left behind him in 1859 has the dubious distinction of being the largest market for slaves in the upper South. There were reportedly as many slave dealers as mule traders in Lexington, with public auctions conducted on the courthouse square and private sales in several buildings downtown. Yet, at the same time, many citizens disfavored slavery. Henry Clay freed the people he had enslaved in his will, and others were granted freedom during their former owners' lives. Lexington had a thriving Black business community.

7
FREE BLACK LEXINGTON

The readers of previous histories of Lexington could be forgiven if they came away thinking there were only three groups of people in Lexington before the Civil War: horsemen, enslaved persons and the people who enslaved them, interspersed with a couple of politicians of stature. Obviously, nothing is further from the truth, but the lives of the various economic levels of people become obscured by the focus of those histories.

Information on free Black people in Kentucky is rare and hard to ferret out. Fortunately, two unpublished master's theses housed at the University of Kentucky illuminate the lives of free Black residents of Lexington in the first half of the nineteenth century, one by Stephen G. Moerland, looking more at community life, and one by Rachel Kennedy, focused more on housing patterns. The authors examined census records, court records, maps and tax records, among other sources. This chapter draws heavily on their works.

Lexington has been described as a haven for free Black people in the antebellum period. As a percentage of the local population, the number rose from a modest 1.6 percent in 1800 to a robust 8.5 percent in 1850. This is in the face of ever more restrictive state and local laws. While the first Kentucky Constitution in 1792 treated free Black and white residents on much the same basis, the second constitution, adopted in 1799, began constricting the rights of the free Black population: they could not vote, could not own weapons, could not testify against a white person in court and could not travel without written proof of freedom. Oddly, this last restriction opened up job opportunities in Lexington when an economic depression in the early 1800s led white laborers, who could travel freely, to leave for better jobs in the growing Ohio River towns.

Free Black laborers held a sizeable proportion of skilled and semiskilled jobs. Men were brick and stone masons, gardeners, grocers, carpenters, wagon drivers, shoemakers and painters. Barbering was a special niche, since that role was viewed as not appropriate for white men, opening the trade to barbershops serving both races. Many barbers, in fact, became well-to-do, owning rental property and their own shops. Women were laundresses, midwives, maids and cooks and even factory laborers in the hemp factories and other businesses, often for lower wages than competing white laborers, which caused friction from time to time. After a local ordinance was adopted in 1832, however, Black people were barred from owning a tavern, coffeehouse or "victualing house," or selling liquor, evidence of a growing concern in the white community over the possibility of "drunken mobs" causing violence.

Freedom was achieved in a variety of ways:

- By grant by an owner (prohibited in Virginia, and thus Lexington, until 1782)
- Born free (rare in Kentucky)
- Never enslaved in the first place (even rarer)
- In exchange for military service by both sides in the Revolutionary War, but particularly by the British
- Purchase of his or her own freedom (owners, particularly those engaged in agriculture where work was seasonal, and for those enslaved persons who had special skills like shoemaking, which were not always in demand, would allow enslaved persons to work for pay elsewhere in the community, by which labor they could save the money to buy freedom)
- And purchase by another family member who in turn emancipated

This last method of emancipation led to some unusual circumstances in which Black people, free or enslaved, owned others and an enslaved person purchased the freedom of a spouse. This was especially the case where enslaved husbands freed their wives because the law in Kentucky was that the status of children was conferred by the status of their mother. Thus buying the freedom of a wife automatically freed their children. An 1850 state law prohibited a Black resident of any status from owning another who was not a parent, spouse or descendant. Another quirk arose with the passage of a state law in 1852 that required a newly freed person to leave Kentucky within one year. To avoid forcing a spouse to leave and divide the family, one spouse might purchase his or her spouse but not emancipate. One impediment to emancipation was proving to the court that the newly freed person would not become a ward of the city, and frequently the court imposed the requirement of a surety bond to be called upon if the individuals could not support themselves. This was rarely a problem for white property owners but more difficult for Black people. Proof of free status was a certificate of emancipation issued by the Fayette County Court. The court met monthly, and Moerland states that at least one certificate was issued at almost every session of the court.

A significant development for the free Black population was the case of *Free Frank and Lucy v. Denham's Administrators* by Kentucky's highest court in 1824, which recognized the right of free Black persons to marry, thus legitimizing families and providing for the right of inheritance, in contrast to enslaved persons, who were not legally permitted to marry.

The free Black population of Lexington actively supported their community, both free and enslaved, by establishing and supporting churches and benevolent societies, including, for example, the Colored People's Union Benevolent Society, formed in 1843, to provide financial assistance to other freed persons, help pay for funerals and supply small stipends to widows. By the 1830s, there were three African American churches independent of white congregations and at least one supported by the Methodist Church, itself a mixed-race congregation. By 1859, a fourth independent church had been established. Most owners of enslaved persons gave them Sundays off work, and even enslaved persons in the rural area would come to town for church and to visit friends and family.

At least one Black congregation, the present St. Paul AME Church, founded initially as a mission of the Methodist Church, was an active station on the Underground Railroad. By 1850, a narrow, twisting flight of stairs had been constructed behind the pulpit, leading to a small room with but a single window to house a freedom seeker until he or she could continue their journey north.

The free Black community followed the general encouragement of education that was a pattern for Lexington at large. By 1844, a school for Black children had been established, with thirty-two attending the first year, and records show thirty-eight in classes in 1850.

The American Colonization Society was formed in 1816 to send formerly enslaved persons to Liberia in Africa. Some supported it as a step toward ending slavery, others as a means of reducing competition for jobs; but only 661 freed persons were sent from Kentucky. The free Black community in Lexington did not actively support the movement.

Residentially, Black households were scattered throughout the community, with at least one on virtually every block. To be sure, most white-owned houses lined the major street, and roads with Black houses were side streets and back streets, but given that almost everyone lived in easy walking distance of their place of employment the general distribution made sense.

There were three significant clusters or enclaves of Black residences, one along east Short Street near the edge of the city, in the vicinity of present Gratz Park and on what is now the South Hill Historic District. In 1859, there were at least twenty-one Black residences in the six-block area bounded by South Broadway, High Street (both sides), South Limestone (Mulberry) and West Euclid Streets. Six of these houses, equal in construction to contemporary white residences, survive on South Hill today. Kennedy concludes there was a clear preference for free Black people to live near one another, and on blocks where the backyards adjoined, there was a freedom of movement through the block without the necessity of interacting with the white population on public streets. While both races interacted on many business matters, outside of that, the races were generally separate. The creation of Black residential areas on the edges of the city was a post–Civil War event discussed in a later chapter.

An example of the financial success some obtained was Samuel A. Oldham, a barber. He was emancipated in 1826, and in only two years, tax records show he owned two horses worth ninety dollars. That a barber, in the city, owned two horses suggests he had additional business on the side employing them. By 1840, he had amassed $9,250 worth of property, a significant sum for the period, including his barbershop, three city lots and a slave.

In 1833, Edward Stout Abdy, a white visitor to Lexington, wrote in a letter that he observed two white women who refused to ride in a stagecoach occupied by two free Black passengers. Instead of removing them, the driver drove on, leaving the white women on the roadside. Abdy wrote, "This little incident shows that the free blacks are too numerous and too wealthy in Lexington to be slighted by the state coach proprietor."

John Kellogg wrote in a paper for the *Journal of Southern History* in 1982 that "the pattern of Negro residence in Lexington in the 1880's was a composite of persistent antebellum enclaves, post war peripheral settlements, and a scatter[ing] of blacks among the white population."

8

THE CIVIL WAR PERIOD

It was in this context that news of the attack on Fort Sumter in April 1861 reached Lexington. The city, and families, were divided in their support for the Northern or Southern causes. Many prominent families saw members join opposing armies, with the fearful prospect that brother could meet brother in battle. Within a week, an armed body of men marched through Lexington carrying a Confederate flag, en route to join the Southern army. Within a month, Lexington banker and Union supporter David Sayre began receiving shipments of rifles and revolvers. He used his bank as a base for secretly distributing them to his friends.

The Union army soon occupied Lexington, camping primarily on the fairgrounds at Maxwell Springs. The first detachment of about 200 arrived on August 21, and, after a brief encounter with Lexington's home guard during which no shots were fired, marched on to camp thirty miles south of Lexington. A month later, 1,500 Union troops arrived at the fairgrounds. The next night, September 20, Captain (later General) John Hunt Morgan and a small band slipped out of town to join the Confederate army in Tennessee. Soon the Fourteenth Ohio arrived in Lexington, and a recruiting office was opened downtown. Although the Northern troops generally held Lexington for the entirety of the war as part of the Kentucky Military District, their presence was not uninterrupted.

CSA general Kirby Smith and his eleven thousand troops moved into Lexington on September 2, 1862, following his victory over Union forces at Richmond three days earlier, and the city responded with a Confederate Thanksgiving Day celebration.

Lexington, however, being Lexington, also continued its Thoroughbred racing schedule. The fall meet at the Lexington Track was held as scheduled in mid-September, and no doubt General Smith and his officers attended the races. This makes Lexington racing notable for two reasons: it was the only "Southern" track that did not halt racing during the conflict, and these were the only races run under the Confederate flag.

An estimated $1 million in food, arms, horses and other property were taken by the Southern forces during this raid, additionally burdening the central Kentucky area after the destruction of supplies and ammunition by the Northern troops as they retreated. Smith's forces did not remain in Lexington long, however, and in early October retreated to Tennessee.

The Union forces promptly returned to their encampments, some five hundred troops of Ohio calvary pitching their tents on Ashland Farm, Henry Clay's former estate, under the command of Major Charles B. Seidel. With the loss of the battle at Perryville, Confederate forces began their retreat again to Tennessee, and General Morgan and his cavalry began conducting raids to distract the Union army and protect the rear of the Southern forces. Late at night on October 17, Morgan learned of Seidel's forces at Ashland, and early in the morning of the next day, Morgan attacked. Variously called the "Battle of Lexington" and the "Battle of Ashland," the encounter lasted only minutes, as Morgan completely surprised his opponents. Some of Morgan's men were detached to pursue about one hundred of the Ohioans who were in downtown Lexington, the officers purportedly imbibing at the Phoenix Hotel. Most of the pursued men took refuge in the courthouse but surrendered after a few shots were exchanged.

The Southerners, however, were not in a position to hold prisoners and, after relieving them of their arms and horses and other supplies, Morgan "paroled" the Union forces on the lawn of Ashland. The act of granting parole during war essentially was an exchange of freedom for those captured in return for their promise not to continue fighting in the war. In practice, it was an act of expediency, and many paroled troops later rejoined their armies.

In a final effort to slow any Union armies intent on pursuing the larger Confederate forces, Morgan burned army stables and the railroad depot before leaving Lexington. An immediate effect of this battle was that the Union army built Fort Clay on the Versailles Road near what is now Angliana Avenue. The fort was not for the purpose of defending Lexington. It was to defend the railroad lines. Lexington was the intersecting point for rail traffic from Cincinnati and Louisville. The Union armies needed tremendous amounts of food and supplies, which were shipped in quantities by rail. If the railroad shipments at Lexington were interrupted, the Union army in the western theater would come to a halt.

That winter, Lexington and the surrounding countryside began receiving Union-supporting refugees from Tennessee, including a large number of escaped slaves. By spring, Camp Nelson in Jessamine County was established for African American Union troops, and in March 1864, formal recruitment of Black soldiers began.

Morgan returned again in June 1864 at the head of 2,700 men, again looking for horses, arms and supplies more than trying to capture and hold territory. They generally looted Lexington, breaking into stores and shops, taking clothing, hats and saddles as well. John Clay, a son of Henry Clay who had inherited a portion of the Ashland estate and maintained a breeding operation there, lost over $25,000 in horses, and Morgan's men relieved the Branch Bank of Kentucky, in Lexington, of over $10,000. After burning several buildings for effect, Morgan headed for Cythaniana. Barely escaping from an engagement there, Morgan and a small group retreated to Virginia. This raid was the end of any military engagements in central Kentucky. Morgan died on September 3, 1864, in a fight near Greeneville, Tennessee.

Seven months later, on April 9, 1865, General Robert E. Lee surrendered at Appomattox Courthouse. When the news reached Lexington, those who favored the Northern side celebrated in the streets into the night with gunfire, fireworks, bonfires and the firing of cannon from Fort Clay. Those who favored the Southern side remained quietly in their houses.

9

A TALE OF TWO—OR SIX—SCHOOLS

In 1865, the entanglement of Transylvania Seminary and the future University of Kentucky began, which spanned several decades and ultimately involved six educational institutions by merger, revival and separation, a story best recounted in one place rather than stretched out chronologically.

Transylvania Seminary was chartered by the Virginia legislature in 1780 and opened in a log cabin in Boyle County. By the end of that decade, it was seeking better financial support and a new location. Citizens of Lexington banded together to purchase out-lot 6 (today's Gratz Park block) and offered it to Transylvania as an inducement to move, which was accepted. Transylvania Seminary opened in Lexington in 1789. Transylvania built its main building on the north end of the lot. That building burned to the ground in 1829. The cause of the fire, revealed years later by Cassius Clay, was that his servant fell asleep while polishing Clay's boots, knocking over a candle.

Bacon College, an offshoot of Georgetown College, was charted by the Kentucky legislature in 1837 and operated for several years until closing in 1851 for lack of sufficient financial support. In 1858, its charter was revived. The school relocated to Harrodsburg and took the new name of Kentucky University.

By 1865, both Transylvania College and Kentucky University were again struggling financially. The end of the war, however, provided an opportunity

Old gate to Gratz Park showing Old Morrison in the background. *Katrina Ockerman.*

to take advantage of a new federal law to save both schools. In 1863, the Morrill Act was passed by Congress to encourage the establishment of agricultural and mechanical colleges by providing federal lands to be occupied by and/or sold to provide funding for what came to be called "land grant" colleges. The Kentucky legislature took advantage of this offer by amending the charters of both educational institutions to merge the two schools under the name of "Kentucky University" and created the Agricultural and Mechanical College under the wings of the combined institution in Lexington. At the same time, Transylvania/KU began a department of religious studies.

The Morrill Act funding was used to acquire a portion of Henry Clay's former lands. The Ashland Estate had been divided between the Clays' two surviving sons and their daughter, with James Clay getting the mansion and surrounding lands and Anne Brown Clay (and her husband, James Erwin) getting what was called the Woodlands, the central component of which is today's Woodland Park. James Clay died in 1864, and his widow, unable to continue running the farm financially, offered it for sale. In total, there were 433 acres immediately adjacent to the town.

The Lexington community viewed these developments with approval, seeing the establishment of the new A&M College on Clay's estate as appropriate and a suitable monument to the statesman. The president of the A&M College occupied the mansion as his residence, and various buildings on the farm were put to use as dormitories, classrooms, and faculty housing. Most of the land between the mansion and town was cleared for farming.

What seemed like an ideal arrangement, however, contained the seeds of discord: the essential conflict between a sectarian school run by a religious denomination and a secular school run by state government.

By 1878, the tensions had become too much, and the two institutions split. The former Transylvania Seminary retained its new name of Kentucky University and retreated to its downtown campus. It also obtained a separate charter for its religious department, now formally the College of the Bible. The state took possession of the farm and informed the A&M College it needed to relocate, first arranging for a two-year lease for the college.

The college opened a statewide bidding process for its favor, being willing to relocate to whichever city would give it the best terms. Louisville and Covington responded and made offers. It can only be imagined how different Lexington's future would have been had the state's flagship university moved to either Louisville, by then Kentucky's largest city, or Covington, across the river from a growing Cincinnati.

However, Lexington was unwilling to lose the only state-sponsored educational institution and proposed to give its fairgrounds as the new site, together with $30,000 in city bonds and $20,000 in Fayette County bonds to be used for buildings, which was accepted. The state A&M College moved to its new home south of today's Euclid Avenue, eventually changing its name to the University of Kentucky.

Three more changes complete the early story of Lexington's major educational institutions.

Hamilton College, founded in 1869 as Hocker Female College and renamed following a major gift from William Hamilton in 1878, was located on a six-acre tract across North Broadway a block north of Kentucky University/Transylvania. It was the first exclusively women's college west of the Appalachian Mountains and, at its most successful, had over two hundred students from thirteen states housed in an impressive four story Italianate brick building. What is known today as Graham Cottage, named for its first president, was also constructed in 1869 as the college president's residence. In 1903, it merged with Kentucky University, which converted it into a junior college. The dormitory was demolished in 1962, but

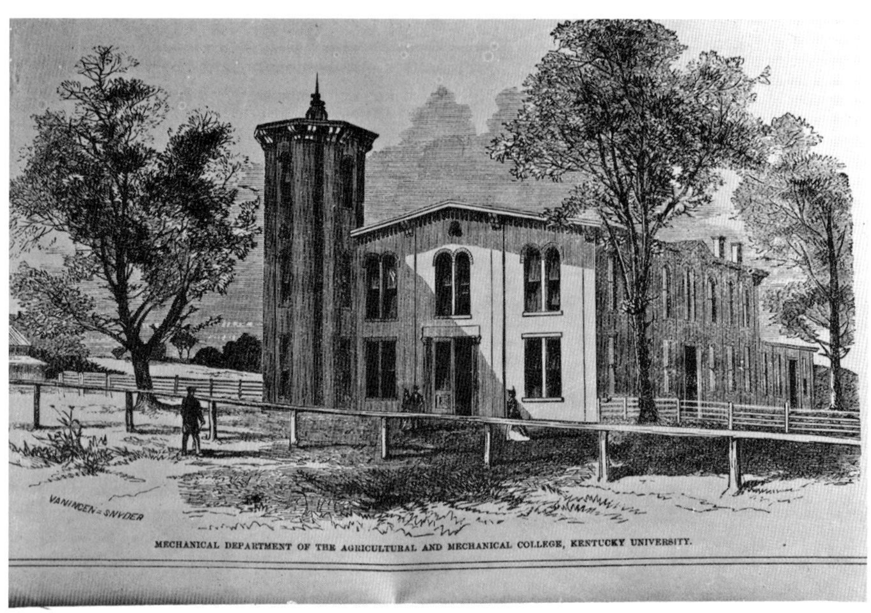

Kentucky A&M College buildings on the Ashland Estate. *Courtesy of the University of Kentucky Archives.*

Graham Cottage, which also served as the residence of four presidents of Transylvania, is used today as its alumni house.

The College of the Bible, the outgrowth of old Bacon College, separated from Transylvania University in 1950 and built its own campus on South Limestone across from the University of Kentucky. In 1965, it took the new name of Lexington Theological Seminary.

Finally, to eliminate the confusion of names between the two major educational institutions, Kentucky University returned to the name of Transylvania University in 1908.

10

RECOVERY AND REDEFINITION

Lexington after the war was at the crossroads of several contrasting trends and events. Physically there was little damage, although the fairgrounds buildings had been burned to the ground by a fire allegedly started by a Union army campfire. Morgan's raiders had burned only a few buildings. But martial law had been declared, and for a time a Union general ran the city. However, Lexington and Kentucky were not subject to the Reconstruction Acts applicable to the Southern states because Kentucky never formally seceded, and the acts applied only to those states in rebellion.

Traditional agricultural markets to the south were devastated, and new markets to the north had yet to be developed. Yet there was a run of new construction and new businesses. The equine industry had been hit the hardest, with hundreds of horses appropriated by cavalry units of both sides. Racing ended for the immediate future in the South, and new competing tracks and breeding farms opened in the North, although racing was never interrupted in Lexington and continued at the Kentucky Association track.

Finally, as is common over history when agricultural activity is disrupted, many people drifted into urban centers, including Lexington. Included in this diaspora were a comparatively large number of newly freed and enfranchised Black people, which led to a change in both the residential patterns of Lexington and the politics of the city.

One immediate effect of the war was the dramatic increase in the number of banks in Lexington. Grinstead & Bradley's Bank opened in 1863, followed by the First National Bank and the Lexington City National Bank in 1865.

The J.M. Hocker & Co. Bank opened in 1868, and Headley & Anderson's Bank, the National Exchange Bank and the Fayette National Bank would open two years later, totaling seven new banks in as many years.

This certainly suggests there was a large amount of investment capital in central Kentucky that was being shifted from other purposes to lending and there were enough borrowers to warrant new banks. A set of new national laws, however, initiated the movement.

In 1863, the National Currency Act was narrowly passed by Congress as a part of the Lincoln administration's plan to take control of and make national matters of currency. Previously, state-chartered banks could issue their own currency, not always fully backed by gold and silver reserves. The actual value of these notes could and did vary from place to place and even among banks in a given area depending on the perceived strength of a particular bank. The act authorized the creation of federally chartered banks and the issuance of a national currency printed by the U.S. government. At the same time, a tax was placed on state banknotes, effectively driving them out of existence.

The following year, the National Banking Act superseded the prior law, also providing for federal chartering of national banks, taking that authority away from state legislatures and converting more than 1,500 state banks across the country to national banks.

Lexington followed the national pattern of converting state-chartered banks and establishing new nationally chartered banks.

The year 1870 saw the establishment of the *Lexington Press* as the first daily newspaper in the community. A second daily paper, the *Lexington Transcript*, started in 1876. The two merged in 1895 and in 1905 began to be published under the banner of the *Lexington Herald*.

As economic activity began to recover during the late 1860s and 1870s, other physical changes were seen in Lexington. The Lexington & Big Sandy Railroad was reorganized as the Elizabethtown, Lexington & Big Sandy in 1869, and the first rails were laid in the new railbed between Town Branch and Vine Street in March 1872. Two new hotels, the Drake and the St. Nicholas, opened in 1870.

Some churches were expanding: the cornerstone for St. Peter's Catholic Church on West Short was laid in 1868, the Pilgrim Baptist Church (eventually Calvary Baptist) was formed in 1875 and in 1877 built a large church on the southwest corner of Upper and Church Streets and First Presbyterian Church erected a new sanctuary on Market Street in 1872. In 1874, the Catholic churches bought fifty-seven acres on West Main, opposite the Lexington Cemetery, and established the Catholic Cemetery.

Other churches, however, suffered from the divisions occasioned by the war as reflected in Lexington life. The Methodist Church in America divided in 1844 over the issue of whether a bishop could enslave people. The Lexington church adhered to the southern branch, although it had a congregation almost evenly divided between the races. When the two national denominations did not reunite after the war, a third of the Methodists in Lexington left Hill (High) Street Methodist Church, South (now First United Methodist Church), to form what became Centenary Methodist, affiliated with the northern branch. At the same time, approximately three hundred Black members of Hill Street left to join St. Paul's, a mission of the Hill Street Church begun in 1820. St. Paul's, in turn, left the denomination to join the national African Methodist Church.

The Presbyterians likewise had divided north and south. First Presbyterian was organized in 1784 and Second Presbyterian in 1815. Each suffered a split, and Lexington had two churches on each side. In this period, the four consolidated into one southern and one northern church.

The war had a major effect on the equine industry in central Kentucky and Lexington. Not only had local breeders lost stock to both armies, but also their traditional buyers of horses farther south lost fortunes and farms, tracks shut down and racing south of Lexington virtually ceased. Even the Louisville track, Woodlawn, had closed for the war, and its infield served as a field hospital for the Union army. Successful breeders like John Clay, Henry Clay's son, had turned north during the war, moving stock out of Kentucky when they could. He took his famous Thoroughbred *Kentucky* to New Jersey to sell. Others moved racing stables to Pennsylvania, New Jersey, New York and even Boston.

The other side of the game was the group of newly rich men in the Northeast who had made fortunes during the war. These men saw investing in horses and horse farms, and building new tracks, as ways to spend their money in competition with one another. The geographic center of horse breeding and horse racing shifted from Lexington to Saratoga. It would be many years before it returned.

The comparatively sudden influx of free Black people into Lexington began around 1863 as both free and the formerly enslaved sought the protection of the Federal army stationed there. It only increased after the war, dramatically changing residential and political patterns.

In 1860, Lexington had a population of just over nine thousand, of which about one-third was Black, and the city limits were set as a one-mile radius from the courthouse (although development did not observe such a clean geometric pattern within and without the limits). Most people lived within walking distance of where they worked, and the races were generally integrated across the community in terms of residence. A study did find a handful of clusters of freed Black residents living near one another, notably in the 300 and 400 blocks of South Limestone and South Upper and on North Upper near Seventh Street. The same study, however, also found roughly two-thirds of the free Black population lived throughout the city, on almost every street.

Part of this mix of living pattern can be attributed to the ease of living near work. Another part has been attributed to a conscious effort by community leaders, not only in Lexington but across the South, of discouraging a grouping of too many African Americans in one neighborhood out of concern, if not fear, of any organized disruptions.

After the war, it all changed. Lexington's Black population, stable for two decades before 1860, jumped from 3,080 in that year to 7,170 by 1870. Some came to Lexington seeking work, some seeking educational opportunities, others seeking benefits from the Freedmen's Bureau. Lexington's total population, itself relatively unchanged for many years, rose from under 10,000 to 14,801 in the same period, illustrating that almost the entire increase in population was due to migration of Black people.

Lexington did not have the housing stock to accommodate an almost 50 percent increase in residents.

Lexington's housing pattern was that of a classic pedestrian city with three modifying factors. The classic pattern is the wealthy elite living in the center and the residents becoming progressively poorer toward the edges of the city. In Lexington, the pattern varied with wealthy living along the major roads into town, relegating poorer white and freed Black residents to less visible side streets. Further, Transylvania University and Kentucky A&M College drew well-to-do residents into their penumbra; in contrast, the less affluent lived closer to railroads and industrial sections. Finally, the rolling land of central Kentucky and Lexington led to well-off residents living on or near the tops of hills and the poor living in low areas prone to flooding.

When over four thousand African Americans arrived, the areas where they settled fit the pattern: along railroad tracks, adjacent to industrial areas and in low valleys with poor drainage along the edges of town. Specifically, ten such clusters have been identified, usually named for the white men who divided property into narrow lots to rent or sell on long terms. Some of these names are familiar today; others have been lost as the areas have been redeveloped.

Brucetown, Taylortown, Smithtown and Kinkeadtown were on the north end, set in undeveloped out-lots used mainly for pastures. Goodloetown (actually comprising three nearby groupings) lay on the east side of town, roughly between today's Maple Tree and the railroad along Winchester Road. Lee's Row was on the west between the railroad and the cemetery north of Main. Adamstown was between the city center and the A&M College along what became Euclid Avenue/Avenue of Champions. Pralltown was between South Limestone and the railroad going out of town to the south, and the Davis Bottom/Lower Street ran along the bottom of the hill below the South Hill and Western Suburb historic districts. Unlike the others, Davis Bottom was a poor Irish settlement before the war, resulting in a generally integrated neighborhood.

By the mid-1870s, Lexington was becoming a segregated community, initiated by this clustering of new Black residents on the edges. Developers, however, rode the trend. Some, like Richard deRoode, an active land speculator, offered lots in 1869 in a one-hundred-lot subdivision for one-third down in cash, but he would sell to Black buyers on credit and no down payment if they produced letters of reference from their employers. Others, like S.N. Drake in the same year, offered forty choice lots with the condition that none would be sold to Black people.

Not all was negative for Lexington's Black community. The same influx led to the formation of several fraternal and benevolent organizations. The Kentucky Grand Lodge of Colored Masons, based in Louisville, started a lodge in Lexington in 1867. In 1872, a Black Odd Fellow Lodge was started. The Black churches also benefitted from new members and even new churches, both congregations and new buildings. The Colored Agricultural and Mechanical Association was founded in 1869 and held its first fair and exposition in the fall of that year. Women of the Black community purchased a building on Church Street, between Limestone and Upper, built in 1824 as a Methodist church, and started the first Black school in what became known as "Ladies Hall." Teachers were provided by the American Missionary Society, funded by the federal government, to promote Black education. Political, educational and economic leadership was concentrated primarily among Black residents who had been free before the war.

Not all of the formerly enslaved moved into the city of Lexington, however. Several rural settlements were created, some by groups of freed families and some by the former owners who desired to keep their labor force near the farm. In the latter case, the farm owners would carve out a section of land

The former Methodist Church, erected 1820, on Church Street. It later became "Ladies Hall." *Courtesy of the Bullock Photographic Collection, Transylvania University Library.*

along a road and divide it into lots, which in turn were either sold or leased to families. Some of these rural settlements or hamlets like Chilesburg have disappeared, either by conversion back to agricultural use or absorption by Lexington when incorporated into new subdivisions, although the names of the roads echo their existence.

A 1971 Housing Report of the Lexington and Fayette County Planning Commission identified seventeen hamlets and historic communities still in existence in Fayette County, as follows:

Athens/Cross Plains | Founded as Cross Plains in 1783 by Samuel Todd and others who came in the wake of Daniel Boone, it was located at the intersection of Boonesboro Road and Cleveland Pike, site of the existing settlement of Athens. Cross Plains started as a religious community by erecting a Baptist church in 1785 at the site now occupied by the Christian Church. The town of Athens was laid out as a village by surveyor Harvey Bledsoe in 1826. Several woolen factories were built in 1836. Because of frequent fires, manufacturing ended in Athens only a couple of years later. In 1840, Athens supported three hundred residents, two taverns, several general stores and two distilleries within a mile of town, plus other shops. It became a place for large gatherings, for gambling, quarter racing on dirt roads and chicken and dog fights. In 1971, the white population was 99 percent of the total.

Avon | Located at the intersection of the L&N Railroad tracks and Briar Hill Pike, in eastern Fayette County. Until recently, Avon didn't have a large enough concentration of buildings to be considered a settlement. The name Avon, in the past, referred only to the farming area owned by the T.J. Weathers heirs. Weathers's daughter and her husband, C.E. Gibson, subdivided their inherited land in 1956, creating Avon Acre, a mainly white enclave.

Bracktown | Located in the northwestern part of Fayette County, it was one of the many settlements subdivided after the Civil War. Before the war, the land now known as Bracktown was owned by Fredrick Braxton, James H. Henderson and the Martin family. In 1887, Robert Stone subdivided the twenty-one acres into long, narrow lots, and he named it Stonetown after himself. He sold this land to African Americans who were able to pay the one-hundred-dollars-per-acre price. The southern part of Bracktown was owned by Reverend Fredrick Braxton, who was the first pastor of an African American church at Main and Merino Street in Lexington, and the inhabitants named their whole village after him, calling it Bracktown.

Cadentown | A settlement in Fayette County east of Lexington established solely for the purpose of providing housing for the formerly enslaved after the Civil War. The farm was owned by Samuel McKee; later residence of Captain John Starks, Revolutionary War officer; and purchased in 1867 by Owen Caden, a farmer born in Ireland in 1830. He came to the United States in 1840, and his children settled in the area, subdividing the land of about seventy acres at the intersection of Liberty and Todds Road. A 1971 Housing Report states that the one-room schoolhouse was still standing.

Clays Ferry | Eli Cleveland, one of the early pioneers who obtained 740 acres of land between Boone Creek and the Richmond Pike in southern Fayette County, founded a settlement called Cleveland in the 1780s. He built shipyards, warehouses and mills on the Kentucky River at the site, which is now known as Clays Ferry. The settlement was populated only by Cleveland and his large number of enslaved laborers until his death in 1829. His will gave 624 acres to his sister Martha and her husband, Bernard Franklin. Eli gave this sister all his estate because of her frequent assistance and goodwill. To his other six brothers and sisters, he left fifty cents each. As the estate was handed down to subsequent generations, it became thoroughly subdivided and now contains about 135 acres as a community, mostly white.

Coletown | Located on Walnut Hill Road opposite Shelby Lane in southern Fayette County, it was one of the few settlements created before the Civil War. In 1843, the will of Sarah Johnson stated that ten acres of land on the Walnut Hill Pike shall be given to Milly Cole, formerly enslaved by Sarah Johnson's brother. In 1868, upon the death of Milly Cole, the ten acres were subdivided equally into three parts for her three children. At approximately the same time, other prominent families in the area were the Spencer Seals family, the Isaacs family and the Tookey family. This twenty-two-acre community contained only thirty people in 1971, and the racial mixture is half Black, half white.

Fort Springs (formerly Slickaway) | In 1826, Major Thomas Streshly, who owned a large amount of land and enslaved many, gave three Black men whom he emancipated some land on the Woodford Road (Versailles Road). These men started the area known as Reform. Enslaved people in the area used to slip away at night for jamborees at Reform, and thus the name Slickaway was established. In 1882, Slickaway was a sizable community with a church and a school attended by the Black population, the South Elkhorn Baptist Church (1859) and a school attended by the white population. There were approximately 150 people living in Slickaway in 1882, twice as many Black residents as there were white. The name Slickaway lasted until 1890, when a prominent resident of the area grew tired of going to Pisgah (two miles away in Woodford County) and had the Fort Springs Post Office created. He named it for the Old Stone Tavern of Lewis O'Neal, built in 1826. It has a large spring that runs under the structure. During the Civil War, the tavern was transformed into a headquarters or fort, thus bringing about the name.

Jimtown | Jacob Sidener Sr. (b. 1788) was the first of the Sidener family to reside in the area. Sidener worked a 20-acre farm in Fayette County for three years to make enough money to buy a 400-acre farm at the site now called Jimtown. He paid three dollars an acre for this land covered with trees. He began to accumulate other property until he had built up an estate of 1,400 acres. He gave half of his estate to be divided up among his eleven children. One of his sons was Jacob Sidener Jr. (1824–91), who resided on a 190-acre farm called Uniondale. James Sidener, the unmarried son of Jacob Sidener Jr., was the founder of Jimtown. In 1888, he sold plots of land (around 34 acres total now) to African Americans at about eighty dollars per acre to start the settlement that bears his name, located on the Greewich Pike and south of Hume Bedford Pike.

Jonestown (formerly Jonesboro) | Located south of Lexington off Tates Creek Road. In 1817, Samuel S. Wilson bought a farm; after the Civil War, he began to subdivide it. In 1883, he sold nearly fifty acres to Thomas Jones, who subdivided it into lots in 1893—the original plat for the Jones Subdivision is in the Fayette County Courthouse. It is a totally African American community of forty-six acres.

Little Georgetown | Located on the south side of Parkers Mill Road in western Fayette County in the area of the large land holdings of the Parker and Waltz families. In the first half of the nineteenth century, this area belonged to George Waltz, who gave some of his two hundred acres to several African Americans, who built their homes there and named the settlement after him—they had to add on the "Little" because there was already a Georgetown in Kentucky. In the early twentieth century, Little Georgetown had a schoolhouse operated by the Fayette County School System. Today around ninety people live in the mostly Black community, which covers thirty-four acres on the south side of Parker's Mill Road.

Little Texas | Located in the western part of Fayette County at the corner of Military Pike and Fort Springs–Pincard Lane. It was established in the early eighteenth century as one of the few all-white rural communities. The area of Shannondale, as it was called when it was founded, was established by several families, those of William H. Davis, J.H. Lushy, Joseph Carter and others. They had a baseball team that traveled to play other teams in a covered wagon. It is said that this produced the nickname "Texas" for the Shannondale residents. The names were used interchangeably up to the 1930s. It covers about seventeen acres.

Loradale | A village in northern Fayette County on the Russell Cave Road, it developed mostly during the twentieth century. Originally owned by Jacob Sidener Sr. and his heirs (as was Jimtown), it was sold and then subdivided in 1904 by the Huffman family. The Old Union Church in Loradale was first built in 1823, rebuilt in 1875 and again in 1927. It is a mainly white community of ninety covering roughly 110 acres, but most of that is farmland.

Maddoxtown | Samuel Maddox was born in Maryland in 1817, and upon moving to Kentucky, he married a woman from Scott County and lived there most of his life as a farmer. In 1871, he subdivided part of his farm on Huffman Mill Road and sold lots to the formerly enslaved. In 1879, he sold off larger tracts of land of approximately ten acres for an average of eighty dollars per acre. In Maddoxtown, these larger tracts were subdivided into smaller lots in the early twentieth century. It supported its own school, which was held in the church erected in 1875. There are about forty-four acres today (of which about twenty acres are used for farming) for ninety-eight people, of whom 75 percent are African American.

Pricetown-Nihizertown-Centerville | These three communities are located close together in the Todds Road and Cleveland Pike area in eastern Fayette County. All three were created around the same time after the Civil War for the development of housing for the formerly enslaved. Willis Price was heir to land left to him by other members of the Price family who came to Fayette County soon after Daniel Boone. Dr. Sanford Price, son of Willis Price, subdivided some of this land to form the settlement of Pricetown. At the same time, John Nihizer was in the process of subdividing his land into two-acre lots, which he sold for eighty to one hundred dollars per acre. The combined population of the three areas is approximately 105, of which two-thirds are Black, and the combined acreage is about seventy-seven.

Spears (formerly Spearsville) | This settlement on the Tates Creek Pike, split by the Jessamine-Fayette County line, was settled in the late eighteenth century by John L. Spears from Virginia. He attracted other settlers because of his education and skill as a surveyor and schoolteacher. It covers about fifteen acres and was settled by white residents.

Uttingertown-Columbus | These two towns are located off of Royster Road just north of Winchester Road, and both were created for the free Black population after the Civil War. In 1869, Samuel L. Uttinger sold several two-acre lots for about one hundred dollars per acre. He later mysteriously disappeared and was declared dead. Next to Uttingertown is Columbiatown, known now as Columbus. Clarence H. Crimm subdivided his land in 1893, began to sell lots at one hundred dollars per acre and chose the name for the Columbian Exposition which had just closed in Chicago. The combined Black population is around ninety.

Willa Lane | Located east of Lexington and south of Avon on the Haley Pike, it was a farming area before 1920 owned by J. Madison Jackson and his wife, Kitty. After her husband's death, Kitty Jackson subdivided her 415 acres into large lots. A man by the name of Goodpaster bought two of these lots totaling 103 acres, and in 1920 he subdivided them into approximately 5-acre lots. In 1924, Willa B. Stevenson bought Goodpaster's land and sold it to African Americans who settled there. There are around forty-three people in the community, covering about 45 acres of land (28 of which is farmland).

In short, economic necessity and private enterprise combined to change a generally integrated Lexington into one segregated by neighborhoods. It was, in the words of one author, largely the accidental result of a combination of impersonal forces: a massive in-migration, scarcity of space in the city core, availability of cheap land on the edges and the poverty of the newcomers, which limited their options. The thousands of new residents did bring one important thing with them—the right to vote. Changes in city politics would follow.

11

BLACK HORSEMEN OF THE BLUEGRASS

Few know that the first professional athletes, as a group, not particular individuals, were African American jockeys. Most learned to ride under African American trainers or other jockeys literally in the farm system of the southern states, riding their owners' mounts on tracks across the South. But only the South—putting a skilled slave on a fast horse in a free state was not considered a good plan. The customary job route was a likely young farm worker would be assigned to the stables. When talent was shown, a former jockey turned trainer would teach the boy to ride. When he became too old, or too heavy, to continue riding, he could become a trainer and complete the cycle.

After emancipation, however, these highly skilled jockeys were free to ride for whomever and wherever they could, and a large number migrated to the northern tracks. Oliver Lewis and others are described in *Race Horse Men* as being "everywhere" in the 1880s. In any event, the southern tracks, horse farms and breeding stock were decimated by the war, which was almost completely fought over that land. The region experienced a 49 percent decline in wealth, and racing shifted to the North and families with wealth who desired to display it.

Thoroughbred racing has been described as America's first and only truly national sport, predating baseball, football, basketball and all others. The *Spirit of the Times*, a national racing publication, reported that by the 1880s, African American jockeys had "almost monopolized the best mounts, and have been singularly successful."

One famous African American trainer was Edward "Brown Dick" Brown, born in slavery in 1850 in Fayette County outside Lexington. Robert A. Alexander bought him in 1857. Brown first rode for Alexander's Woodburn Farm, then trained. As a slave, Brown rode the famous *Asteroid*. After he was freed, he remained at the farm. As a jockey, he won the Belmont aboard *Kingfisher*, who was trained by another famous African American, Raleigh Colson. After Alexander's death, Brown trained for Daniel Swigert, former Woodburn farm manager, and trained the 1877 Kentucky Derby winner *Baden-Baden*. Brown would later be elected to racing's Hall of Fame.

What follows are profiles of six famous African American jockeys.

Oliver Lewis

Oliver Lewis won the first Kentucky Derby in 1875 on *Aristides*. Of the fifteen horses in the race, all but two were carrying Black jockeys. *Aristides* was part of a two-horse entry by owner Hal Price McGrath, whose strategy was for Lewis to ride out to an early and fast lead to tire the competing horses, then pull back to allow his favored horse, *Chesapeake*, to win. Aristides, however, did not comply with Lewis's efforts to restrain him, and *Chesapeake* was in the middle of the pack. McGrath waved to Lewis to go for the win, and he did, in the fastest time to date for a three-year-old horse carrying only one hundred pounds. The other horse finished eighth. A $105 ticket in the auction pools paid $495; McGrath won the $2,850 purse and a sterling silver punch bowl valued at $1,000.

Lewis and *Aristides* nearly won the Belmont Stakes the next month, but McGrath was following his same strategy and ordered Lewis to defer to another McGrath horse. He did, and McGrath collected some $30,000 in bets. Lewis reportedly quit riding at some point and became a bookmaker. Lexington would name a new street Oliver Lewis Way in time.

Isaac Murphy

Murphy's year of birth is disputed, varying from 1856 to 1864. Mooney asserts he was born into slavery, while Hotaling says he was the freeborn son of a Union soldier who was at Camp Nelson on the Kentucky River, having enlisted in 1864. He was named Isaac Burns, but upon his father's death in the 1860s, his mother moved back into her father's house with Isaac and his sister. His grandfather was Green Murphy, and young Isaac took his last name as his own.

After starting work on a horse farm as an exercise boy, Murphy went to work for noted Black trainer Eli Jorden at age twelve. Two years later, he rode in his first race in Louisville just five days after Lewis won the first Kentucky Derby. He finished last. The following year, he won at Lexington, and his career was taking off. In 1877, he won in his debut at Saratoga and continued that year to win the St. Ledger at Louisville, the Breckinridge Stakes at Pimlico and other races. In 1879, he was second in the Kentucky Derby.

In that same year, Murphy engineered a come-from-behind win over two more favored horses in the Travers at Saratoga. After the race, he was interviewed by a writer for the *Spirit of the Times*. Hotaling details the interview over several pages where Murphy describes the strategy he used to slip up on the other jockeys in the race to judge their mounts' stamina without making them think he was a threat. The race was for a mile and three quarters, and his winning time just over three minutes, but as Hotaling described it, "He turned moments into something almost like leisure, racing up, dropping back, feeling out the competition, adapting tactics, and keeping a sharp eye on his colt." The writer concluded Murphy was "one of the best jockeys in America." His record that year to the date of the interview showed it: thirty-five races, twenty-two wins and one tie.

The 1880s witnessed a boom in the horse racing world as new money made in mining out West made wealthy men who entered into the field. Murphy was riding for many wealthy men and their stables and was able to dictate the terms of his riding contracts. He married in 1882 and bought a small house on Megowan Street in Lexington. The next year, they bought what some described as a mansion on Third Street. It had ten rooms with a rooftop observatory from which he could watch, and scout, his human and equine competition running at the nearby Kentucky Association track. Murphy had his own carriage and a white valet. He and his wife did not sell their first house but kept it as rental property.

With annual earnings of $12,000 in 1887, Murphy was, according to Hotaling, America's highest-paid athlete. At one time he was paid $10,000 a year by one owner just to be "on call." In 1890, he won the Suburban in New York on *Salvator*, beating a rival named *Tenny*. The defeated horse owner demanded a rematch, which was scheduled for Coney Island in June. Murphy won by a head. The next month, the rivalry continued at new

Monmouth Park in New Jersey. It was another win for Murphy. Two weeks later, a large party was held to celebrate the victories, attended by Murphy and the white elites. He was at the top.

The fall came two days after the party, when he appeared drunk and barely able to stay in the saddle in a race, coming in last and even falling off his horse before the finish. People in the crowd rushed the track to catch his horse and put him back on to trot to the finish. Friends carried him to the jockeys' locker room and hurried him away.

Controversy followed Murphy from that day on. Theories flew that he had been drunk or that he had been starving himself so much to keep his weight down that he had not fully recovered from the party. Murphy always maintained he had been poisoned and was never well after.

The following January, however, and probably back up to his "winter weight," he and his wife gave a large party at their Lexington house attended by Oliver Lewis. That May, Murphy won his third Kentucky Derby. He won a respectable thirty-two races that year, but only won six times in forty-two races the next year. Rides on quality horses were decreasing.

Starting in 1893, Murphy bought some two-year-old horses and tried his hand at training but was not successful. He still raced, but the question of his drinking followed him. He readily admitted that, if he won "it was all right," but if he lost or had a poor mount, it was due to drinking.

On February 12, 1896, he died of pneumonia at his home in Lexington. His lifetime record was 628 wins in 1,412 races, a 44 percent win record, which still stands. When the National Museum of Racing and Hall of Fame was established in 1955, Murphy was the first jockey inducted.

James Winkfield

Jimmy Winkfield was born in a small community east of Lexington in 1892, and by the time he was fourteen he was hired to work horses at Latonia. The next year, another horseman, Bub May, hired him as a jockey. In contrast to Murphy's $10,000-a-year retainer, Winkfield was paid $10 per month plus board. Winkfield improved with each race and won 40 races at an Indiana track. May gave him a three-year contract with an increase in pay to $25 per month and sent him to race in New Orleans. He raced third in the 1900 Kentucky Derby, and in 1901 May sold Winkfield's contract to Patrick Dunne. Winkfield's star continued to rise as he won 161 races and was first in the Derby.

Racial tensions were also rising in the racing world, and Winkfield was involved in what was called a "race war" at the Chicago track where white jockeys, jealous of the successes of Winkfield and other Black riders, initiated some incidents on and off the track. The Black jockeys pushed back, and track officials had to intervene.

For the 1902 Derby, Thomas Clay McDowell, a Henry Clay descendant, hired Winkfield to ride *Alan-a-Dale*, which he did for the second back-to-back Derby win since Isaac Murphy (1890 and 1891). McDowell gave him a $1,000 bonus. The following year, he finished second in the Derby. He never rode in the Kentucky Derby again and stands as the only African American to win the Derby in the twentieth century.

An event in the 1903 Futurity at Sheepshead Bay was life changing. Lexington's John E. Madden asked Winkfield to ride for him, and Winkfield agreed. Then Bud May offered him $3,000 to ride for May. Winkfield switched, which infuriated Madden. Madden's horse was third, while Winkfield finished sixth. Madden told Winkfield that if he wouldn't ride for him, Madden would see to it he rode for no one. Madden had the influence to enforce his statement, and Winkfield's rides dropped by almost half the next year. The next year he left for Europe and won the Warsaw Derby, starting his European career.

By 1910, Winkfield's riding in Europe and Russia had become so successful he stopped even trying to ride in the United States. His American wife sued him for abandonment and divorce, which he did not contest. He started riding for the owner of the largest stable in Poland, an Armenian oil baron. By 1917, he was the leading jockey for Czar Nicholas II and lived in a luxurious apartment across from the Kremlin with a Russian wife and a white valet. He had won the Warsaw Derby twice, the Russian Derby four times, and the Emperor's Purse. In fact, he won all three of Russia's derbies—Moscow, Warsaw and St. Petersburg—a sort of czarist Triple Crown.

In 1917, the Russian Revolution and the Bolsheviks took a dim view of what Mooney called "a man who made an opulent living piloting the playthings of the rich." Winkfield, his wife and three children and stable hands walked 262 of the finest horses in Europe to safety in Poland with a loss of only 10 animals, a journey of 1,100 miles.

Winkfield continued on to France, where he returned to riding and winning, including the Prix du President de la Republique, the Grand Prix de Deauville and other major races. By 1930, when he retired from riding, he owned his own stable and horse farm outside of Paris in Maisons-Laffitte.

He had a lifetime total of 2,300 wins. The outbreak of World War II forced the Winkfield family to retreat to the United States, but they returned to France in 1953. He remained in France until his death in 1974.

James "Soup" Perkins

James Perkins was born in Kansas City in 1880, but his family soon moved to Lexington. His father worked with trotters and eventually not only James but also three of his brothers went into the horse business. They lived very close to the Kentucky Association track, and by age ten James was working at the stables.

At that time, he started riding and by thirteen he was earning $4,000 per year. In two more years, Perkins doubled that figure, winning Lexington's Phoenix Stakes, and followed that by winning the Kentucky Derby. Within another year, he was making enough to buy his family a brick house.

He gained the nickname "Soup" from other boys around the Lexington track before he began racing. He frequently walked home for lunch and, on his return, when asked what he had to eat, he always said, "Soup."

By 1895, Soup Perkins was the leading jockey, with 192 wins.

Unfortunately, his career took a dramatic turn down, and in 1897 he was disqualified from racing at the Northern Kentucky track. In two more years, his racing career was over. He died in 1911. In 2011, Lexington named a street for him: Soup Perkins Alley.

Willie Simms

According to Hotaling, Willie Simms ran off from his home in Georgia to get into racing because he liked the colors of jockey silks. He was born in 1870 and at age twenty-one won the 1891 featured race Spinway at Saratoga. He was the fifth leading jockey that year, rising to second the next year. This earned him a $12,000 per year contract from wealthy businessman and horseman Pierre Lorillard.

In 1893, Simms won the Belmont Stakes and was the number one jockey in the country with 182 wins. The following year was a repeat: won the Belmont, top jockey. This led to multiple contracts with horsemen and trainers lining up, in order, for his services. He earned about $20,000 a year as one of the wealthiest jockeys in America.

Simms gave racing in England a try, the first American jockey to race there; but few mounts came his way and he returned to Morris Park after only four months and won the Kentucky Derby in 1896. This was the first year the winning horse was draped in a blanket of roses, although the nickname "Run for the Roses" would not be coined for two more decades.

Over his career, Simms won the Belmont twice, the Derby twice and the Preakness once, in 1898, making him the only African American jockey to win all three Triple Crown races. He retired in 1901 with one of the best all-time win records and died in New Jersey in 1927.

Alonzo "Lonnie" Clayton

Hotaling calls Lonnie Clayton no less than a boy wonder, the youngest jockey to win the Kentucky Derby. Born in Kansas City, Kansas, in 1876, Clayton, his family and eight brothers and sisters moved to Little Rock in 1886. Two years later, he ran away from home to join a brother working as a jockey in Chicago. Two years later, in 1890, he moved to New Jersey and began his riding career. The next year, he won his first stakes, the Champaign at Morris Park. This was followed in 1892 by the Derby victory, which he won at age fifteen.

Clayton won many races during that decade, riding across the country, winning the Kentucky Oaks twice and finishing in the money three more times in the Derby. He also won the Monmouth Handicap in 1893 and the Arkansas Derby in 1895 and finished third in the 1896 Preakness. He won 144 races in 1895 alone. Like other successful Black jockeys, Clayton became an "employment center" and employed as many as four full-time Black employees.

However, he, too, encountered career-ending trouble. In 1901, he was arrested for trying to fix a race. The charges were ultimately dropped, but the damage to his reputation was done. At the same time, the Jim Crow era's rising racial prejudice and a trend toward favoring white jockeys meant fewer opportunities for jockeys like Clayton. The 1896 U.S. Supreme Court decision in *Plessy v. Ferguson* endorsing the concept of "separate but equal" treatment furthered the trend.

Clayton retired, but unable to continue earning money as well as he had, he sold properties he had acquired and moved to California, where he worked as a hotel bellhop. He died there in 1917 from tuberculosis.

End of an Era

Several social trends conspired to thwart Black jockeys. Not only *Plessy* inspired and approved segregation but a spate of Jim Crow laws in the South, a movement to restrict Black athletes in many sports and the popularization of racial determination promoting the white, Anglo Saxon race as superior did as well. Beyond those trends, however, were the activities of the Ku Klux Klan and restricted chances for advancement, which drove African Americans away from the rural settings, where a boy could become familiar with horses, into the cities. Finally, the influx of more wealthy men, who acquired larger and larger tracts of land, drove out the small Black horsemen who were the traditional starting points for future jockeys. The era of dominance by Black jockeys ended.

In Lexington, however, they are still honored. Streets have been named for Lewis and Perkins. Murphy has memorials at the Kentucky Horse Park and African Cemetery No. 2 and has a Memorial Art Garden near where his house was. Lewis, Clayton, Murphy, Perkins, Simms and Winkfield and others are featured in original portraits painted by a local artist, Adalin Wichman, in an equine display encircling the atrium of the Lexington Public Library main branch.

12

PROGRESSIVES AND BOSSISM

Before the Civil War, there was a general deference to the economic and professional elite. Henry Clay and John C. Breckinridge, successively, dominated local politics. Clay and the Whig Party were dead. Breckinridge, absent from Lexington and Kentucky for the duration of the war as a Confederate general and secretary of war, then in exile in Cuba, Europe and Canada for three more years, did not return to Lexington until the spring of 1869, after President Andrew Johnson declared a general amnesty. When he did, his health was not good, and he refused all requests to run for office again and participated little in local politics. He died in his house on West Second Street on May 17, 1875.

In the place of patrician politics, Lexington saw the rise of "boss" politics like that of Tammany Hall in New York City. Instead of being centered in a lodge hall, it was centered on a grocery store.

The grocer was Dennis Mulligan, born and orphaned in Ireland and an immigrant to New York City at age seventeen in 1834. There he was given a job by the mayor and introduced to politics and patronage. By 1837, he was working for the Long Island Railroad and surveying future lines in Lexington. By the 1840s, he had established a successful grocery business downtown, married and become involved in politics. In 1866, just as the war ended, he was elected to the city council.

Mulligan's grocery store, on the northeast corner of Vine and Upper Streets, became the gathering place for job seekers and politicians. Although Mulligan never gained control of all of Lexington, he did secure a majority

Dennis Mulligan. *Courtesy of the University of Kentucky Archives.*

of the city council members to his side. When Lexington was incorporated in 1831, the charter provided that the council would appoint the mayor, and it was through this stratagem that he achieved effective control of the government. In addition, to secure his base, Mulligan worked himself into the position of control over the hiring of members of the police and fire forces. Through his contacts in the railroad industry, he also was able to secure jobs in the yards for his supporters. His political machine came to be known as "Mulligan's Ring."

While Mulligan was quick to favor city expenditures that benefited him or his supporters, he generally obstructed municipal improvements. Perhaps the best example of the former was his sponsorship of the erection of a new city market house, Jackson Hall, in 1879. It was located across Limestone Street from his own grocery, giving him quick access to market goods. The city government had its offices on the second floor, so he was steps away on a daily basis. He even arranged that the front of the market building would be set back from the street ten feet, to better expose his store to the public.

Jackson Hall itself was a large two-story brick structure covering the entire block bounded by Limestone, Upper, Vine and Water Streets. P.L. Lundin, a Swedish architect who was located in Lexington and who designed several buildings downtown, designed the building. The first floor had inside stalls on either side of a central aisle. It would be demolished in 1941.

At the same time, Mulligan favored stagecoaches over expansion of the rail system and opposed the introduction of telephones because he objected to the number of poles required. He also opposed relocating the state capital to Lexington and was the only negative vote when the question of providing funding to keep the Agricultural and Mechanical College in Lexington came before the council.

Lexington had long been served in its water needs by a system of wells, springs and cisterns. The cisterns were located at major intersections below the streets and drawn upon in the event of fire. Many residents would have their own cisterns under their front yards for the same purpose. Unfortunately, privies were often located too close to or upstream from these cisterns, resulting in outbreaks of typhoid fever and other diseases. Mulligan, however, adamantly opposed the city establishing a municipal waterworks as a solution. Finally, a group of businessmen started a private water company, and Mulligan even opposed the city contracting with it.

Evidence of his success in business—and he had other businesses beyond the grocery—and politics came when he built what is known today as Maxwell House, the residence of the presidents of the University of Kentucky, for his son. He also helped elect his son to the general assembly, where he was useful in blocking legislation Mulligan opposed. His son, James H. Mulligan, would have a successful career as a lawyer, legislator and judge and pen the famous poem "In Kentucky." In the final line, he describes Kentucky politics as "the damnedest." He came to that conclusion, no doubt, from observing his father's machine.

By the late 1870s, however, at the height of Mulligan's power, a group of reform-minded councilmen began to challenge him, led by Calvin Morgan, brother of General John Hunt Morgan, and Lexington's first German and Jewish councilman, Moses Kaufman. By 1880, the reformers had achieved a change in the city charter to have the mayor elected by popular vote over Mulligan's opposition, thus stripping him of much of his power. The first popularly elected mayor, Charles M. Johnson Jr., was a reformer and began leading the way for city improvements. Mulligan opposed taking street maintenance out of the hands of the mayor and putting it under the authority of a paid engineer for the simple reason he would lose patronage positions. When a reworking of one street was proposed, Mulligan favored hauling off the old rock and buying new, a move that failed when it was revealed that one of Mulligan's friends, the keeper of the workhouse, would be paid for removing the old rock and bringing in the new. The council voted to reuse the existing rock at substantial savings.

In a bid to regain power, Mulligan ran for mayor against Johnson in 1884 and was soundly defeated. Election of the reform mayor Henry T. Duncan in 1893 and 1899 showed the community no longer supported Mulligan and his machine. When he died in 1901, it appears his machine effectively died with him.

While Mulligan and his machine were controlling city hall, other aspects of Lexington showed that the recovery from the war and the immediate postwar period was happening. The year 1870 saw the opening of two new hotels, the Drake on Short Street between Broadway and Mill and the St. Nicholas on East Main west of Limestone. The National Exchange Bank was chartered in that year, as was the Fayette National Bank. The *Lexington Press* newspaper started publication late in 1870, and the *Lexington Transcript* followed in 1876. The two merged in 1895, eventually becoming the *Lexington Herald*.

The religious community was also at work. In the early years of the decade, First Presbyterian Church sold its building on Broadway to what became known as Broadway Christian Church, whose members had left Main Street Christian. First Presbyterian built a new church on Mill Street.

The Catholic church established Calvary Catholic Cemetery in 1874, across the road from the Lexington Cemetery. In 1875, a second Baptist church was formed, named Pilgrim Baptist, which would become Upper Street Baptist after it built a church at Upper and Church Streets and then, in 1904, Calvary Baptist Church after a move to High Street.

The first Jewish institution was the Spinozo Society, a burial society, founded in 1872. It bought a tract of land on Tates Creek Road for a cemetery. However, the land proved to be too far from town, and the road there was either muddy or frozen or otherwise too difficult for families to attend burials. That land was sold in 1885 and the graves moved to a section in the Lexington Cemetery. The tract on Tates Creek Road is now the site of Cassidy and Morton schools.

A B'nai B'rith Lodge was started in 1877. The *Lexington Leader* reported a meeting of the Ohavay Zion Association in May 1903, although the congregation would not incorporate until 1912. Temple Adath Israel was organized in November 1903.

In 1877, the Sisters of Charity of Nazareth founded St. Joseph Hospital on Linden Walk, near Maxwell. Twelve years later, the Woman's Guild of Christ Episcopal Church founded the Protestant Infirmary, which would become a community hospital governed by representatives of all of the non-Catholic faiths and renamed Good Samaritan Hospital.

In 1876, the Kentucky Agricultural & Mechanical Association purchased sixty-two acres off South Broadway and built a grandstand and racetrack, known as the Fair Grounds and today known as the Red Mile harness track. Floral Hall, an octagonal building, was built in 1882 to house flower shows. The Fair Grounds hosted trotting horse races, fairs, circuses and carnivals and other events.

The year 1879 was the centennial of the founding of Lexington, and on April 2 that city had a large celebration, starting with a one-hundred-cannon salute, continuing with a mile-long parade through downtown and concluding with speeches in Morrison Chapel at Transylvania.

The chamber of commerce was established in 1881 and began promoting Lexington as the "Queen of the Bluegrass." For a city of almost twenty thousand residents, there was much to promote. There were ten newspapers (three daily), twenty-three educational institutions, a growing number of churches and hotels, a telephone company and an electric company, railroad service to three depots (the C&O and the L&N depots were in downtown, the Cincinnati Southern on South Broadway near the Red Mile fairgrounds), eight banks, free mail delivery (1883) from the new post office,

Southern Railway Station, South Broadway. *Public domain.*

although rural delivery would not begin for six more years, and mule-drawn streetcars. The mules would be replaced in 1890 by electric streetcars, which in turn would be replaced by buses in 1938. In 1882, however, the mule cars conveyed residents to the new Woodland Park. The Woodland Park Association purchased 110 acres of the former Henry Clay estate, sold off lots to finance the project and built the park on 15 acres in the center with a large auditorium and a lake.

The old courthouse was razed in 1883 and the new one completed in 1884. It was described in its plans as two stories high, with basement and a dome, 90 by 117 feet and 100 feet tall. Standing in the center hall below the dome was Joel T. Hart's famous statute *Woman Triumphant*. The courthouse and the statue would be destroyed by fire in 1897.

Other major fires plagued Lexington. In 1875, a fire consumed all the buildings on the east side of Limestone between Short and Main Streets, and several structures along Short Street. In 1886, the Odd Fellows Hall, known as the Opera House, also burned. The present Lexington Opera House on Broadway was built in response and opened the following year.

The later part of the nineteenth century, largely through the advent of rail lines and the progressive city administrations that followed the Mulligan era, saved Lexington from being just another rural agricultural community and made it into a major center for business and commerce. What Lexington had lacked in waterway transportation was replaced by rail. By 1900, the

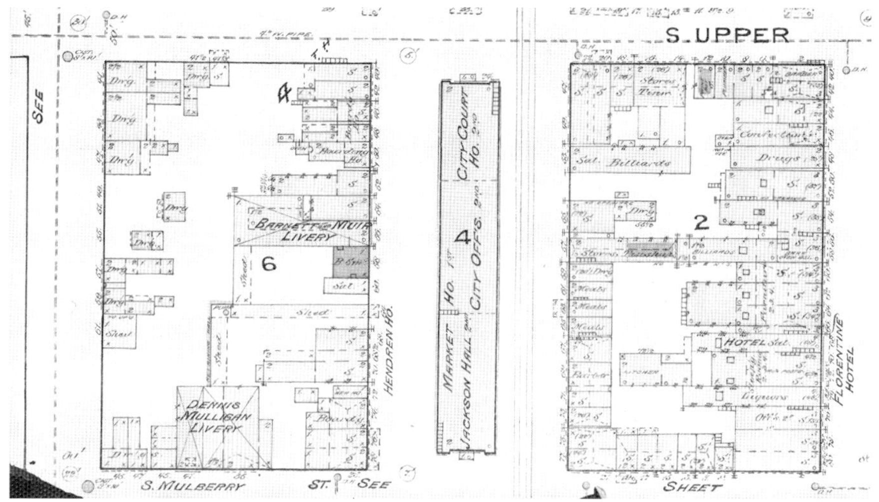

Lexington 1886 Sanborn Map showing the Market House/City Hall between Upper and Limestone Streets. *Public domain.*

population had grown to roughly twenty-six thousand. The end of the century also marked an unusual "war" of sorts.

The toll roads, privately owned by various corporations, still existed, and it still cost to travel outside of the city, although generally, preachers, doctors and funeral processions were not charged. Beginning in 1898, an attack on toll roads began, as much as anything for the reason the roads were not always well maintained. Nighttime bands of horsemen began attacking the toll booths, burning some, tearing down the toll poles across the road and even attacking the booth operators. By the end of the 1890s, counties were able to purchase rights to the roads at bargain prices, and control of the roads passed from private control to Fayette County and the state.

The early years of the twentieth century also witnessed another transportation revolution in Lexington. In March 1905, the C&O, L&N and Lexington and Elizabethtown Railroad companies proposed building a new Union Station on Main Street if the city would construct a viaduct over the tracks from Main to High Street. In turn, the railroads would complete the enclosure of Town Branch.

The first viaduct opened in 1907, and the easier access to the south of town led to the development of residential subdivisions along Rose Street and in the present Aylesford Place subdivision.

By 1913, two more viaducts were under construction in the west end, one extending Jefferson Street over the tracks to High Street and another over the L&N tracts connecting Main Street and Leestown Road, thus providing better access to the cemetery. In 1914, the newspaper reported an estimated five thousand people a day were using the Jefferson Viaduct, and Lexington's first "business loop" was now complete, allowing traffic to travel Main, Harrison (now King), High and Jefferson without fear of being stopped by a train.

The demise of Dennis Mulligan and his machine did not mean an end of boss-style politics in Lexington, however. Largely with the support of Kaufman and other local reform leaders, as well as the young members of the Democratic Party, William "Billy" Klair was elected to the statehouse in 1899, the beginning of his reign as a political leader and later unchallenged boss of Lexington's politics.

13
ALL THE GOOD VICES

Klair's rise coincided with the "progressive era" of American history, when reform leaders at every level sought to clean up politics, improve public health and morals and enlarge educational opportunities. In several ways, the progressive movement had its effects on Lexington, and because it was Lexington, it involved women, whiskey and horses.

Billy Klair rode the reform movement to power as machine politics and patronage supplanted the saloon politics of Mulligan's time. Somewhat counterintuitively, Klair cemented his control during the progressive era even though one of the primary tenets of the movement was to remove figures such as him from government. He did not support every reform proposal and actively opposed some, but he was a major player for three decades, first in Lexington and then in the state. For that reason, Klair appears and reappears in the telling of Lexington's history.

Another major player, locally and nationally, was Madeline McDowell Breckinridge, who was born in 1872, just three years before Klair. A great-granddaughter of Henry Clay, she was married to Desha Breckinridge, editor of the *Lexington Herald* and son of a cousin of former vice president John C. Breckinridge. Together, this couple advocated reform causes in Lexington and beyond. Her sister-in-law was Sophonisba Breckinridge, another well-known reform leader and, in 1892, the first woman admitted to practice law in Kentucky. Her father died in 1899 and left her with income from a trust, which gave her the financial freedom to pursue her goals.

Left: Billy Klair. *Courtesy of the Lexington Public Library.*

Right: Portrait of Madeline McDowell Breckinridge, by Ella Sophonisha Hergeshiemer. *Courtesy of the University of Kentucky Archives.*

The winter of 1899–1900 in Lexington was unusually cold, and many suffered. At this time, the city had no organized community charity to respond to the need. The mayor called on Madeline Breckinridge and other women in the community to organize a new system, and as a result, she was a co-founder of both the Associated Charities of Lexington (1900) and the Lexington Civic League (1901). The former, as the name suggests, worked to coordinate relief efforts in the community and advocated for the casework method of public assistance.

The Civic League focused on the creation of public parks, public kindergartens and manual training in schools, compulsory school attendance and child labor laws. Through her sister-in-law, by then a professor at the University of Chicago, Madeline Breckinridge was able to bring many of that city's leading progressives to Lexington to give lectures. Largely through her efforts, Kentucky enacted laws establishing a juvenile court system in 1906.

Breckinridge's most important effort, which she exerted on the local, state and national levels, was to promote giving women the right to vote. Women's suffrage was a major goal of the national progressive movement. The theory was that women, voting out of purer motives then men, would reform elections and government, but for her it began in Lexington. Kentucky had given limited voting rights to women—Black and white—in school board elections since before the Civil War, which were made unrestricted in 1894. Breckinridge's efforts to promote universal suffrage brought her into conflict with Billy Klair.

Although Klair supported reform movements when it suited him, he was never an advocate for Black rights. By 1902, he had come to see the right of Black women to vote in the school board elections as a threat to his political control of school system jobs. It does appear to be the case that Black women took greater advantage of their rights than white women. One supporter of Klair's asserted that in the 1900 elections, only about 700 white women voted compared to over 1,700 Black women. Klair introduced a bill in the legislature to repeal the law giving women that limited right to vote.

Breckinridge, her distant cousin Laura Clay (daughter of the abolitionist Cassius M. Clay) and other Lexington women organized to oppose the bill. Under this pressure, Klair proposed a substitute bill, which would, instead of outright repeal, impose a literacy test as a qualification for voting (another way of achieving his goal of excluding Black women from voting). However, the substitute failed, and the original measure passed both houses by substantial majorities and became law.

Breckinridge helped lead a movement to restore the voting law and, in the 1908, 1910 and 1912 legislative sessions, actively lobbied members as the legislative chair of the Federation of Women's Clubs, at the same time becoming active in the national suffrage movement. In this, she parted ways politically with Laura Clay, herself a national leader. Breckinridge wanted a national solution granting women the right to vote; Clay favored addressing the same goal on a state level. In Kentucky, however, their efforts were joint.

Klair felt the pressure not only from the women but also from the pages of Desha Breckinridge's newspaper. In 1910, Klair lent his support to passage of a law giving mothers as well as fathers equal rights in the care of their minor children and putting the question of guardianship in the case of divorce in the hands of the courts. Finally, in 1912, again with Klair's support (for by then his influence was such that he could have killed the bill if he opposed it), women's rights to vote in school board elections were restored.

Breckinridge turned her attention fully to the national issue, serving as president of the Kentucky Equal Rights Association from 1912 to 1915 and again in 1919. She also served as vice president of the National American Woman Suffrage Association from 1913 to 1915. She began receiving invitations from other states to speak on the issue and after 1915 was a nationally ranked speaker. The Nineteenth Amendment to the U.S. Constitution was formally proposed in June 1919, and Breckinridge campaigned actively for its adoption. Kentucky ratified the amendment in January 1920 largely due to her efforts, becoming one of only four southern states to do so. The amendment itself was adopted by a sufficient number of states and became law on August 18, 1920.

Breckinridge attended the International Women's Suffrage Association meeting in Switzerland that year and, upon her return to Lexington, was working on the proposal to rename and repurpose the Kentucky Equal Rights Association into the League of Women Voters. Breckinridge herself, however, was able to exercise her new right to vote only once, in the 1920 November elections. On November 25, she died following a stroke.

The Nineteenth Amendment was not the only one adopted during this era. In 1913, the Sixteenth Amendment settled the legal question of whether the national government had the power to enact income taxes, and the Seventeenth took the power to elect U.S. senators out of the hands of state legislatures by providing for popular elections (which, of course, raised the stakes on the question of women's rights to vote).

Six years later, the Eighteenth Amendment, banning the manufacture, transportation and sale of alcoholic beverages, became law. The effects in Lexington were immediate, both before the effective date as citizens hastened to stock up on liquor and after, when distilleries, bars and saloons closed and people lost jobs.

Distilling corn whiskey, which became known as bourbon whiskey, began as early as the 1770s in Kentucky and was widespread a decade later. The actual driver of distilling was not a thirsty populace but transportation economics. A packhorse could carry only four bushels of corn, but convert the corn to whiskey and the same horse could transport the equivalent of two dozen bushels. In 1780, James E. Pepper opened a distillery in Lexington on the Frankfort Pike next to the Town Branch, and within a few years, a distillery was likely to be found anywhere a good, clear and regularly flowing stream or spring could be found.

By the 1890s, Kentucky had 172 distilleries in operation and produced over one-third of the distilled spirits in the nation. Many of these distilleries were in Lexington and, primarily due to the combination of Town Branch and the main railroad tracks running near each other west of town, were concentrated in what is today called the Distillery District along Manchester Street, the local portion of Old Frankfort Pike. The proximity of the railroads made shipping easier.

Right: Lexington Roller Mills on South Broadway, roughly the site of Triangle Park. *Courtesy of the University of Kentucky Archives.*

Below: Jas. E. Pepper & Co. Distillery and warehouses. Town Branch runs past the site. *Courtesy of the University of Kentucky Archives.*

JAS. E. PEPPER & CO., DISTILLERS—Lexington.

Fayette County Courthouse, 1884–1897. *Courtesy of the Barton K. Battaile Collection.*

In the early 1900s, Lexington's distilleries were producing more than 36,000 barrels of bourbon each year, and because the bourbon would be aged for a number of years before sale, there were sufficient bonded warehouses to store over 180,000 barrels at a time.

By 1910, all but twenty-four of Kentucky's counties had voted "dry." The vote in Lexington in 1914, however, was dominated by the "wets," who won 6,695 to 3,431. For the next six years, Lexington was an oasis of sorts. In the few blocks between Limestone and Jefferson Streets, for example, there were approximately 150 saloons or other drinking establishments.

With enactment of the Prohibition amendment, which took effect at midnight on January 17, 1920, almost all of this came to an end. Distilleries were closed down and warehouses locked. By the time of the adoption of the Twenty-first Amendment, which repealed the Eighteenth, in 1933, only the Pepper warehouse was still in business, limping along through the sale of bourbon for medicinal purposes. The laws during Prohibition did provide for a medicinal exception to sales, and it became common for doctors to

Burned shell of the 1884 courthouse. *Lexington History Museum, John Malik Collection.*

write prescriptions for bourbon to be filled by druggists, who became the primary commercial source of liquor.

The final thrust of the progressive era to affect Lexington, after women's rights, morals and liquor, was an attack on gambling in general and parimutuel wagering at racetracks in particular.

After the Civil War, Thoroughbred breeding and racing in Kentucky suffered. Enormous numbers of horses were stolen by each side during the conflict, the southern tracks shut down, many breeders left the state and the new northern money began to invest in new tracks and horse farms in the New York and New Jersey area.

Lexington and central Kentucky horse interests worked long and hard to return any focus here, even bringing in Colonel George Armstrong Custer as a publicity stunt. Many articles were written for newspapers and other publications extolling the virtues of central Kentucky. Finally, in 1885, August Belmont moved his breeding operation to Lexington, which began the return of the Thoroughbred industry. He started the trend of establishing the large breeding and racing farms we know today. Lamon Harkness purchased Walnut Hall Farm in 1892; James Keene purchased land that had once been in the Breckinridge family, the birthplace of John C. Breckinridge, and named it Castleton Farm the same year; William Collins Whitney began racing in the late 1890s; and John E. Madden established Hamburg Place Farm in 1897. About the same time, Arthur B. Hancock began Claiborne Farm.

In 1884, Black jockey Isaac Murphy of Lexington won the first of his three Kentucky Derby races. He was so successful a rider that he bought a brick mansion on East Third Street that had a third story balcony overlooking the Kentucky Association racetrack.

While this great influx of money and horses was going on in and around Lexington, the progressive reformers were attacking gambling. In the 1890s, New Jersey banned racing, followed by Missouri, Kansas, Tennessee, Washington, D.C., and Louisiana. In 1897, the United States boasted 314 working racetracks. As a result of the successes of the progressives, that number fell to only 25 tracks in 1908. August Belmont managed to stave off a ban in New York by getting a compromise bill approved that banned only off-track betting; even there, however, he could not completely stop the trend, and New York joined the other states with a ban in 1908.

In Kentucky, pro-racing interests took another tack, working in the legislature to create the Kentucky Racing Commission to lay down rules for racing and to assign noncompetitive race dates to the tracks. Churchill Downs was preserved. The Kentucky Association Track in Lexington had closed in 1898, not because of antigambling laws but as a result of the financial panic of 1893, which drove many breeders out of business and, in the process of selling their farms and liquidation stock, flooded the horse market, driving down prices. The overall effect forced the track to close. It reopened in 1905 after new investors appeared, a return to racing in Lexington only possible because the reform effort to ban the sport had failed in Kentucky.

Among those asserting their political influence to benefit racing, breeding and Lexington was political boss Billy Klair. The main issue in the 1927 campaign for governor of Kentucky was gambling. The Democratic candidate proposed to ban it. Klair was a lifelong Democrat and had ensured many party victories in Lexington, but now he had to choose. He chose the horse industry and broke ranks, supporting the Republican. Klair, in his last major political play, carried Lexington for the Republican candidate for governor, who carried the state. Klair's influence and effect on the outcome

City Fairgrounds, circa 1892. *Courtesy of the Barton K. Battaile Collection.*

can easily be seen by the fact that in all of the other statewide offices the Democratic candidate prevailed in Lexington.

The Republican Herbert Hoover was elected president the next year, followed by the market crash of 1929. The Republicans had the power in Kentucky and the nation, and Billy Klair had bolted from his party. He had arguably saved the Kentucky and Lexington horse industry at the cost of his political career, and his influence rapidly diminished from this time.

Women had the vote, the distillery business in Lexington was effectively ended even though Prohibition was repealed, prostitution as a semiofficially condoned business was over, racing was protected and the horse industry had returned.

The population was now over forty-five thousand; less than 30 percent was Black. Sixty passenger trains a day—a day—arrived and departed at the city's two passenger depots over three railroad lines. Additionally, a good number of freight trains served its three railroad freight depots. There were five streetcar lines and seven motor bus routes. The interurban rail lines also carried passengers, usually with hourly departures during the day, to all neighboring towns.

PHOTOGRAPHIC GALLERY

Opposite, top: Downtown Lexington looking east from Broadway at Main Streets, late nineteenth century. *Public domain.*

Opposite, bottom: The Phoenix Hotel. *Courtesy of the Barton K. Battaile Collection.*

Above: Lobby of the Lafayette Hotel, now the Urban County Government Center. *Courtesy of the University of Kentucky Archives.*

Fourteen turnpikes radiated from downtown, which, coupled with three federal highways, served the almost sixteen thousand licensed motor vehicles, a 186 percent increase in just ten years. If any of these vehicles was traveling north–south through Lexington's downtown, it had to stop frequently for the many trains, as all crossings were on grade. The only exceptions were the Harrison or Jefferson viaducts, but that required traveling east or west a few blocks.

Almost eleven thousand families lived in some 9,500 dwellings, only a few hundred of which were duplexes. There were only a handful of what would be considered as apartment houses. The children of these families attended segregated schools. There were eight elementary schools for white children to four for Black, two white junior high schools to one Black and the same number each of high schools.

14
DEPRESSION

The Great Depression, so devastating to much of the country, had a lesser effect on Lexington, which was still tied economically to its agricultural base. Tobacco farming alone, with its seasonal jobs planting and harvesting, helped avoid the worst of the jobless effects. Whatever else the nation gave up, it did not give up cigarettes, and the warehouses along South Broadway still held their sales, although the prices were lower.

True, the Fayette National Bank failed, but First National Bank took over its assets and customers. The mayor called for community leaders to come together in 1930 to raise money for indigents. The universities and the school system cut salaries, and the county closed its orphanage and placed some forty children in private homes.

At the same time, however, positive events were happening. Lexington adopted its first comprehensive plan for regulating zoning and development and also changed its form of government to the city manager model. The University of Kentucky hired a young twenty-nine-year-old as its new basketball coach, and Adolph Rupp began his forty-two-year career in Lexington.

The federal government allotted Lexington $300,000 in relief funds, which were used to rebuild the viaduct over the railroad lines from Main to High Streets in 1931. This meant that there was easy access from High Street to the Union Railroad Station, and as a direct result, the Kentuckian Hotel was built on High Street at the north end of the bridge, opening in 1933.

Above: Segregated and separate grandstand for African Americans at Keeneland Race Course. *Lexington History Museum, John Malik Collection*.

Right: W. Jefferson Harris, first manager of the Junior League Horse Show. *Family photograph.*

That same year, Swift & Co. opened a meat processing plant, and construction began on the Federal Narcotics Farm, providing more jobs. The following year, the new federal courthouse on Barr Street opened, and WLAP Radio, the city's first commercial station, began broadcasting.

The venerable Kentucky Association racetrack in northeast Lexington had been struggling economically for several years, and the condition of its buildings had suffered. The fall meet was canceled in 1930, and the track closed for good in 1934.

It only took two years, however, for horsemen to reach an agreement on the location for a new track; acquire the Keene Farm on Versailles Road; convert the buildings into a clubhouse, grandstand and barns; and open Keeneland Race Track in 1936.

The Standardbred horse world saw the first Lexington Junior League Horse Show at the Red Mile in 1937, begun by local women to raise money for charity. Its first manager was W. Jefferson Harris, a Lexington resident but nationally known Standardbred writer, bloodstock agent and inventor of the breed's Sire Rating System.

Lobby of the Phoenix Hotel, 1900. *Lexington History Museum postcard collection.*

Purchell Department Store, World War II display. *Lexington History Museum, John Malik Collection.*

Effectively, the Depression was over for Lexington.

In 1940, the city and county jointly purchased 523 acres on Versailles Road to construct an airfield, today's Blue Grass Airport. In 1942, the U.S. Army took control of the airport for military operations. Control was returned to local authorities in 1945, and the following year the first terminal was completed and commercial passenger flights began.

When World War II began, the city had a population of just under fifty thousand, with roughly an equal number living in the county. Of that number, over ten thousand registered for the draft. In 1942, the U.S. Army opened the Lexington Signal Depot, a $3 million project to coordinate army installations in the Ohio River Valley. In addition to the construction work, the depot brought several thousand defense workers to Lexington. It also saved Transylvania, which was enduring a steep decline in enrollment due to the war. It avoided closing when the army rented a school building in which to train radio operators, while the air force housed two hundred cadets on campus.

With the shortage of men to fill jobs, the women of Lexington and Fayette County came forward to drive taxis and buses and work in the manufacturing plants, including the new, larger facility of Irving Air Chute Co., which made parachutes for the military.

Women also harvested tobacco, but they were not enough. At the request of local farmers, some six hundred German prisoners of war were sent to Lexington in 1944 and 1945 to help with the tobacco harvest.

15
BOOM TIMES

There was no shortage of people after the war, however. Both universities saw soaring enrollments and significant expansions of their respective campuses. The University of Kentucky went from about three thousand students in 1944 to over ten thousand by 1950.

Two more commercial radio stations were broadcasting, and Wolf Wile and Stewarts Department Stores opened downtown. The city itself was also growing, primarily to the southeast along High Street/Tates Creek Pike. In the late 1940s, Lexington's first suburban shopping center, then known as the Ashland Shopping Center, was built on the north side of Euclid Avenue anchored by a new movie theater. As more stores and shops moved to the block, it took the name Chevy Chase Shopping Center after the residential subdivision of that name on its south side.

Much of the residential growth, unfortunately, was unplanned in the sense of orderly municipal expansion of utility and sewer service, but a strong opposition to the expansion of Lexington voted down efforts to annex portions of the county, a problem that would continue in one form or another until the eventual merger of the city and county in 1974.

The Ashland Theater, however, was not the only new theater. In 1948, the Lyric Theater, with over nine hundred seats, opened on Third Street near a major Black shopping center. Whereas the Ashland facility was for film, the Lyric hosted many famous bands and performers, including Count Basie and Duke Ellington.

Original Guignol Theater building, University of Kentucky, after a fire destroyed it. *Lexington History Museum, John Malik Collection.*

The year 1956 saw a significant development that would have a great effect on business in Lexington and its continued growth. The Lexington Industrial Foundation was formed by local businessmen for the purpose of securing land for new businesses and then making the case for attracting them to Lexington. The foundation bought 139 acres on the north side of the city and invested in bringing utilities and sewers to the site. Its members also made the decision not to seek "smokestack" industries, only "clean manufacturing," a decision that allowed Lexington to avoid the industrial air pollution which would plague other growing communities.

The combined efforts of city leaders, the chamber of commerce and the foundation paid off. IBM selected Lexington for its new electric typewriter plant, which opened in 1956, and brought 250 families from New York to town, in addition to local hires. By 1958, Square D, Dixie Cup and Trane had opened new facilities, and R.J. Reynolds Tobacco Company bought 283 acres south of town for twelve new tobacco warehouses. Between 1954

Alumni Gym, University of Kentucky. *Katrina Ockerman.*

Memorial Coliseum, University of Kentucky. *Katrina Ockerman.*

Above: The Harry James Band in concert at Joyland Park. *Courtesy of the Barton K. Battaile Collection.*

Opposite: Fire on East Main Street. *Lexington History Museum, John Malik Collection.*

and 1963, employment in Lexington increased 260 percent. Enrollment in city schools during the 1950s increased by one-third, and in the county enrollment more than doubled. Voters, however, twice rejected an increase in school taxes needed to handle the growth, and schools were crowded. Relief would not come until a tax increase finally passed in 1962, leading to the construction of eleven new schools in five years.

Two other reactions to growth occurred in 1958. Lexington adopted its urban service boundary, a line around the city outside of which no development would be allowed, the first such enactment in the nation. And the Gratz Park neighborhood was designated as the city's first historic district as preservationists began to work to save significant structures from demolition. The trend toward creating historic districts together with the growth of the two universities effectively blocked the expansion of the business core of downtown.

City population was now over 60,000, a 20 percent increase from before the war, and the county stood at almost 132,000 people, a 30 percent increase in the same period. In 1958, *US News & World Report* listed Lexington as one of the fourteen fastest growing cities in the country.

Lexington's churches responded to the rapid growth as well. Epworth Methodist built a new church on North Limestone in 1950 and Southern Hills Methodist, a new congregation formed from First Methodist downtown, built a new church on Harrodsburg Road in 1959. In 1960, a group from the Baptist Church at High and Woodland bought twenty-two acres on Tates Creek Road to start Immanuel Baptist Church, dedicated in 1962. Another group from the same church established Central Baptist Church on Nicholasville Road. The mother church was renamed Woodland Baptist Church and remained in place. In 1964, Felix Memorial Baptist moved to North Broadway beyond New Circle Road and was renamed Parkway Baptist. It sold its old church to Shiloh Baptist, a Black congregation. And in 1967, Christ the King Catholic Church was built on ten acres in a new subdivision behind Morton Junior High School on East High Street.

The growth in churches and congregations in Lexington was sufficient to attract Reverend Billy Graham, who conducted one of his famous crusades, lasting four days, in UK's Memorial Coliseum on Euclid Avenue and in the football stadium across the street.

16

SEGREGATION, CIVIL RIGHTS AND INTEGRATION

If things were generally quiet in Lexington in the first half of the 1960s, forces were in motion that would lead the last half of that decade to more than make up the difference. The Kentucky Court of Appeals ordered the merger and integration of public schools, transportation changes coupled with urban renewal changed the face of downtown and the growing unpopularity of the Vietnam War erupted on the University of Kentucky's campus.

Congress passed the Civil Rights Act in 1964, and under its authority courts began to order the integration of public schools across the nation. Kentucky was no different. What was somewhat different in the case of Lexington, however, was that the court not only ordered integration to take place but also ordered the merger of the Lexington and Fayette County public schools to aid the process. It is generally agreed in Lexington that what followed was poorly planned and unskillfully executed, and not all of the changes were welcome, even by the Black community.

The original Paul Laurence Dunbar High School, named for an African American poet and located on the north side of downtown, was the Black high school. Built in 1923, it was the first Black high school and only one of eight in the old South to be accredited by the Southern Association of Colleges and Schools. It was the pride of the Black community, both for its academics and athletics. Legendary basketball coach S.T. Roach (1956–65) led his teams to two state championships and six regional championships.

The Dunbar High School boys basketball champions. © *The University of Kentucky, courtesy of the John C. Watt Lexington-Herald Leader Photograph Collection.*

The school board, rather than send white students to Dunbar, elected to close it and distribute its students among the other high schools. This move deeply angered the Black community.

Due to a shortage of buses, however, it was not possible to accomplish an even distribution at once. As a consequence, almost all Black students were sent in the fall of 1967 to Henry Clay High School, then housed on East Main Street. It was said Henry Clay went from forty Black students to 40 percent Black in one year. Although a Black vice principal was named to help with the transition, and homerooms, classes and teams were integrated, there were effectively two schools within one building as each race staked out its hallways and bathrooms.

The next year, the school board proceeded with its plan to spread out the Black students by sending some to Lafayette, Tates Creek and Bryan Station High Schools. However well intentioned, however, this aggravated the situation. It is often the case that a high school boy will have a girlfriend a class or two younger, and that was true of many Black Lexington high schoolers. Busing to the other schools often resulted in each member of a couple in a different school. When the final busing plan took effect for the 1969–70 school year, Black students who had been together in junior high were now spread across the county in four high schools. It was not unusual for young Black men to skip school or leave their school early and make their way downtown to Henry Clay to await their girlfriends.

A further unfortunate effect of integration was to take Black student leaders and neutralize them by making the percentage of each race in each homeroom roughly equal. Because representatives to the student council at Henry Clay were elected from each homeroom, and each homeroom had a white majority, the student council was entirely white from 1967 to 1970. Following the example on college campuses where Black student unions were forming, Black students argued for a Black student council, one afternoon leading a vocal but nonviolent demonstration on the front lawn of Henry Clay.

The school administration was stymied, but the students devised a solution. A group of student leaders from both sides, including the author, who was then student council president, met to discuss the situation. Ultimately, a student meeting was called in the school auditorium as an open forum. The solution agreed upon by all was to amend the bylaws of the council to elect representatives from each academic class—senior, junior and sophomore—which gave the Black students the ability to pool their votes and elect representatives. School elections that spring produced the expected results.

This was not, of course, the end of racial tensions through the school system, but in time inequities were erased and integration of the schools succeeded. As though to close a page of history, the following year the new Henry Clay High School opened on Lakeshore Drive and the Main Street building was remodeled into new offices for the county school administration. A new high school, opened in 1990, revived the historic name of Paul Laurence Dunbar.

Throughout this period of troubled race relations, a calming influence was Harry Sykes, a teacher at the old Dunbar, who was the first Black man elected to the city council, in 1963, serving four terms. He was elected mayor pro tempore (vice mayor) in 1967. He also served as city manager.

17

THE INTERSTATES ARRIVE AND THE RAILROADS GO

Changes in the country's transportation systems in the 1960s affected Lexington and, had a couple of decisions gone another way, could have had disastrous effects.

Passenger service through Lexington by rail had been diminishing for some time. In 1959, the Lexington & Ohio passenger station on the southeast corner of Mill and Vine Streets was demolished. The next year, Union Station on Main Street at the Harrison Viaduct was torn down. Ten years later, the Chesapeake & Ohio (C&O) passenger station at Rose and Vine would also come down. The Southern Railroad Station on South Broadway would survive for several years longer until falling victim to a fire, but it stopped passenger service in the 1960s. The last passenger train left Lexington for Washington, D.C., on May 1, 1971. Freight trains, however, continued to ply their way through downtown; as time would show, freight traffic would shift in large part to the new interstate highways. It was impossible to leave the Fayette County Courthouse and travel in any direction except north without encountering railroad tracks and that due only to a trestle over North Broadway. The danger to Lexington from the drop in rail traffic of both kinds was that it would no longer be the nexus of two major transportation arteries, running north–south and east–west, which had fueled much of the town's growth.

At the same time, the interstate highway network was slowly moving its way toward Lexington. In 1960, Lexington's Urban Renewal Board recommended postponing a decision on the interstate routes for further consideration. Tentative plans for Interstate 64, being constructed east from Louisville, called for the highway to pass several miles north of town. The downtown business community was concerned that consumer traffic from eastern Kentucky, long drawn to Lexington, would pass it by in preference for easier access to Louisville or Cincinnati. Many were advocating a downtown route.

The effect of the intersection of two interstates in Fayette County, instead of elsewhere in the state, cannot be overemphasized. What the Ohio River did for Louisville, the interstates would now do for Lexington. What was fortunate for Lexington was that the routes of Interstates 64 and 75 crossed near Lexington, instead of, say, the state capital of Frankfort. Otherwise, as former mayor Foster Pettit put it in a 2012 interview, "Lexington would have been left a sleepy little college town."

But first the route for Interstate 64 had to be decided. There were three alternatives: north of town, through downtown parallel to Main Street (which required removal of the railroad tracks, another proposal under consideration) or through the deep blocks between High and Maxwell Streets. Both the second and third proposal had the highway entering Lexington from the west either down Old Frankfort Pike/Manchester Street (the second idea) or Versailles Road (the third) and exiting along or over Winchester Road. Land speculators busily bought many parcels of land on the possible routes, and others contemplated the opportunity, together with the urban renewal program, of running the highway through and eliminating poor areas of town. One plan, in fact, proposed a large cloverleaf of exit ramps for the Davis Bottom neighborhood, a historically poor area between South Broadway and Versailles Road along the Southern Railway tracks, which would have extinguished it.

In 1952, when he was first elected mayor, Fred E. Fugazzi began considering the removal of railroad tracks from downtown. This consideration continued under Mayor Shelby Kinkead with the help of city attorney Foster Ockerman and the support of the chamber of commerce; Mayor Kinkead contacted the railroad companies to open discussions. However, a 1956 feasibility study conducted by the C&O Railroad at his request estimated the cost, including land acquisition, construction of five overpasses and eleven underpasses, reimbursement of the railroads for relocation expenses and so on, to exceed $20 million. The idea was set aside as too expensive.

Mayor Fugazzi was reelected in 1964 and, even before taking office, began a series of discussions with community leaders about reviving the idea and approaching it in a more formal fashion. During the intervening decade, economic prospects for the railroads had changed, and it was thought they might be more reasonable.

The interstate route between High and Maxwell was the first to be discarded, leaving the Vine Street route or the northern route, and Vine Street was not viable without removing the tracks.

In 1964, a group of eleven architects and engineers came together to work out a plan for a new downtown on the assumption the tracks would be removed. By 1967, the plan had been adopted by the zoning commission as the official plan for redevelopment of downtown.

This Downtown Plan correctly identified several problems or disadvantages: too little parking for the increasing number of vehicles; vehicular conflicts where roads and railroads met; building obsolescence where old and aging buildings were not suitable for future use or were, like the mills and warehouses along the tracks, no longer appropriate once the tracks were removed; and an overall appearance problem presented by "garish" signs on buildings projecting over the sidewalks, sprawling trashcans lining sidewalks and a "jungle of traffic direction controls." It called for a "vigorous and sincere program of revitalization" to prepare for an anticipated additional seventy thousand people in Lexington by 1980.

Visionary in scale, it called for new parking garages, underground utilities, sign regulations and, interestingly, a system of overhead pedestrian bridges or pedways to connect the major downtown retailers—Purcells, Stewarts, Embry's—and the Phoenix Hotel with the new garages. The pedway proposal is ironic because the plan called for a permanent structure of enclosed bridges connecting retail establishments that were already doomed. Turfland Mall opened in 1967 as Lexington's first enclosed shopping mall, the same year the plan was adopted, opening the exodus of retail from downtown. Fayette Mall and Landsdowne Shopping Center opened in 1971. Lexington Mall opened in 1975. Stewarts and Embry's moved to the new centers. Purchells went out of business in 1971. Within a few years, before the pedways could have even been built, all the retail connector points were gone.

The plan also called for an expressway to run west to east through the new corridor to be reopened by removal of the tracks and a new civic center on the block bounded by Upper, High, Mill and Water/New Vine Streets. The expressway (in reality, the second I-64 proposal) would have entered Vine from High Street, cutting through the present location of Rupp Arena, and exited down what became Midland Avenue when the tracks in that corridor were removed. Various citizen groups, however, continued to oppose the idea of an expressway. State highway officials, to the contrary, were not as concerned about an east–west expressway through downtown as they were about a north–south expressway through downtown. It was opposed by the University of Kentucky, which lay in that proposed route's path.

It is well to pause a moment in the relation of these events to contemplate what Lexington might have looked like had all the expressway plans been achieved. If only I-64 had cut through the Vine Street corridor, the north side of Lexington would have been physically cut off from the developing south in a way more permanent than the railroads. Already, the downtown retail was moving to the south. In the late 1970s, when the County Clerk's Office was forced out of the courthouse by the need for more room for the court system, there was a brief discussion of moving it to Fayette Mall. It didn't happen then but likely would have if the majority of the population needing to license vehicles and record deeds and mortgages was across a limited access highway. The banks would have followed, which would mean the real estate law firms would, too, leaving only the courts north of Vine Street. Downtown would have ceased to exist and a new government and banking/office center erected elsewhere, likely along Reynolds Road when the Reynolds Tobacco Company closed its large complex of tobacco warehouses. If the state plans for running I-75 through downtown had succeeded, downtown would have been drawn and quartered into nonexistence.

While the plan was making its way to formal adoption, Mayor Fugazzi pursued the railroads. He and his advisors developed a step-by-step approach to secure, first, community support, then railroad support, then development of a plan. Again, the railroads were asked to study the problem and, in February 1965, presented their report to the city council. This time the estimated cost was roughly $1.3 million, a fraction of the estimated cost nine years earlier, suggesting that this time the railroad companies saw a benefit from the idea. The multiple overpasses and underpasses would be eliminated, as would be the crossings at eleven streets. While the city felt it could reasonably finance relocation costs, federal help was needed for land acquisition.

The solution was to amend the Urban Renewal Plan to include approximately eighty-two acres downtown to be opened for redevelopment, redirecting urban renewal from residential slums to the new Vine Street corridor. Redevelopment, perhaps elimination, of the Pralltown, Davis Bottom and Irishtown neighborhoods was removed from the plans. Despite a court challenge, the mayor and council moved forward with planning. Ultimately, the Court of Appeals (then Kentucky's highest court) approved the change. The final cost would be an estimated $5.6 million, of which the city would contribute only $1.4 million. Of the eighty-two acres, 40 percent would be developed into new streets, 37 percent of the buildings in the area would be razed and the rest would be rehabilitated by owners. In July 1966, the city commission ratified the Downtown Track Removal Contract, signed by the commission, the railroads and the Urban Renewal Commission. Removal of the tracks, acquisition of land, demolition of buildings and speculation over and jockeying for position within the land area began.

In 1968, the Urban Renewal Commission announced plans for a civic center, not on the three-acre block at High and Upper but on an eleven-acre site west of Broadway. Consultants had recommended a larger area to accommodate a 2,500-seat auditorium/performance hall and sixty thousand square feet of exhibit halls. The consultants specifically ruled out a sports facility as part of the plan, but talks continued between the city and the University of Kentucky about the possibility of both a basketball arena and a football stadium next to the civic center. Stoll Field, the university's football stadium on Euclid, was aging and small by then standards, and the basketball program had outgrown Memorial Coliseum. In 1974, construction began on a $40 million civic center complex to include a hotel and what became Rupp Arena. The football stadium would

Ceremony pulling the first spikes from the downtown railroad tracks. Mayor Fred Fugazzi is in the center wearing a scarf. © *The University of Kentucky, courtesy of the John C. Watt Lexington–Herald Leader Photograph Collection.*

be erected on University of Kentucky land, part of the old Agricultural Farm, on Cooper Drive in 1976.

In 1973, Water Street was officially closed and title conveyed to the Urban Renewal Commission. As a point of historical curiosity, the original Water Street ran from Limestone west to where it was swallowed by railroad tracks west of Broadway. The present Water Street runs east from Limestone to just beyond Rose Street.

Prior to this time, the major banks had all clustered around the courthouse: Bank of Commerce at Main and Cheapside, First National at Main and Upper, Security Trust at Mill and Short, Citizens Union at Upper and Short, New Union Federal at Market and Short, Second National on Cheapside, Lexington Federal on Short between Market and Upper and Central Bank at Upper and Short, the larger banks being the primary tenants in large office buildings. With the advent of the redevelopment of downtown, it was as if all anchors had been cut loose and the banks began to look for new advantageous locations.

Citizens Union was the first, acquiring the block at Upper and High formerly intended for a civic center, erecting what is known today as the "gold bank building" for the color of its windows. First National and Security Trust, whose merger was finally approved after years of litigation in 1968 to form First Security National Bank, acquired land to the east on Main at Harrison (now King) Street for its new building. The Bank of Lexington acquired and erected a uniquely curved building on the northeast corner of new Vine and Limestone, which is now one of the urban county government buildings, the Bank of Lexington having later moved into the "big blue tower" before its acquisition by Fifth Third National Bank out of Cincinnati. Bank of Commerce built a new building farther east on Main than First Security at Rose Street. Lexington Federal, primarily a residential lender, purchased property out on Nicholasville Road at Jesselin Drive to be nearer the new residential subdivisions but maintained a small office downtown. First Federal would occupy one of the new buildings on Vine, as would Central Bank, which took over the site of a failed hotel at Vine and Broadway for its new headquarters.

Two pieces of Lexington's transportation situation remained to be resolved: the completion of New Circle Road and a decision on where the interstate/expressway would run. New Circle opened its last link, between Harrodsburg and Richmond Roads, in 1969, allowing the complete circumnavigation of Lexington. Resolution of the expressway route would await the next city elections in 1971. When Foster Pettit, elected mayor in that year, was asked in an interview for this history what happened to the downtown option, he said, "I stopped it." (A mayor was not the only office holder who could affect highway plans. In the late 1970s, when it was proposed to extend Newtown Pike through Davis Bottom to connect with Euclid, avid opposition from both his loyal voters in Davis Bottom, whose neighborhood would be destroyed, and affluent voters in Chevy Chase, whose neighborhood would be inundated with traffic, inspired Lexington state representative Bill Kenton to stop that plan.) With opposition from city hall to a downtown expressway, the northern route was assured, and Interstate 64 opened officially in 1973, running through northern Fayette County, in part together with Interstate 75. Lexington would have five exits off the system, and the community grew out to the highways.

18

EXPANSION

By 1970, Lexington had grown to a population of over 108,000. Fayette County as a whole had over 174,000 residents. New subdivisions were the order of the day, as was the emergence of the apartment community, clusters of two- or three-story buildings around a pool and clubhouse or other amenities. Good Samaritan Hospital announced new construction estimated to cost $9 million; Central Baptist Hospital contracted for a $5 million expansion. Transylvania University added a $2.8 million science center, and UK began construction on a $6 million animal sciences building and the new VA Hospital.

In the midst of this growth, on May 6, 1970, the antiwar students on the University of Kentucky campus erupted into a large and vocal demonstration. Governor Louie Nunn called out the National Guard, and the ROTC (Reserve Officer Training Corps) building burned to the ground, although the cause was never determined. Off campus, however, the Fayette County military draft boards reported high volunteer enlistments.

On June 24, 1971, new Vine Street officially opened, and the one-way paired streets of Main and Vine and Upper and Limestone were instituted to channel traffic. Now, the longer process of the Urban Renewal Commission of sorting through the titles to real estate, buying or condemning real estate in the corridor, receiving and assessing proposals for development and generally guiding the renewal process could begin. While Citizens Union National Bank would begin construction of the "gold bank" in this year, it was several years before the majority of new buildings would be erected.

Above: A student protest in downtown, 1969. *Courtesy of the University of Kentucky Archives.*

Opposite, top: Looking west along the railroad tracks from the Harrison Viaduct, 1956. *Courtesy of the C&O Historical Society.*

Opposite, bottom: Looking west along Vine Street in the former right-of-way of the railroad, 2013. *Foster Ockerman Jr.*

That the city's population now exceeded 100,000 persons presented a problem for government. The law at that time required that a city with that many people be classified by the legislature as a "first-class city." Lexington was, at the time, a "second-class" city. The only city of the first class in Kentucky's history was Louisville, and over the decades many laws were passed for first-class cities only—meaning custom legislation for Louisville—including the aldermanic form of government.

Lexington's leadership had three choices: do nothing and allow the legislature to reclassify it as a first-class city, seek to increase the threshold number for becoming a first-class city or do something completely different.

They chose the latter and proposed something unheard of in Kentucky and rare in the country: a merger of the city and county into one governmental unit. It was all the more unusual because in Kentucky, Lexington was a municipal corporation created by act of the legislature while Fayette County was a creature of the Kentucky constitution. Special legislature would be required to even authorize the process to begin, and city representative Bill

PARKING

Community Trust Bank

McCann and county representative (and former county judge) Bart Peak co-sponsored a bill in the 1970 General Assembly to allow second-class cities and their counties to merge and become an "urban county." It passed and was signed into law.

Under the Peak-McCann bill, the first step was a citizen petition, and in the summer a citizens group began collecting signatures calling for the creation of a Merger Commission to draft the charter. By year end, the number of signatures was attained and presented to the county clerk, the County Fiscal Court and the City Commission. By the end of March 1971, the city and county had each appointed fifteen persons to the Merger Commission. Due in part to some opposition on the City Commission, the drafting moved slowly. However, in the fall of 1971 Foster Pettit and a new slate of city commissioners were elected, strongly in favor of merger. One of Pettit's first acts as mayor was to appear before a legislative committee in Frankfort and urge it not to take action reclassifying Lexington, but to let the experiment with merger have time to be completed. In January 1972, the city appointed ten additional people to the commission, and with the new members, the commission accelerated its work and presented the proposed charter for the Lexington–Fayette Urban County in June.

The merger movement now undertook the public campaign for ratification of the charter at the November election. Efforts in other cities across the country showed the difficulty of achieving passage. Usually, the county officials opposed a merger because they would lose power. Lexington was fortunate that County Judge Robert Stephens supported merger, even though the county judge would become a minor official in the new government, as would all members of the Fiscal Court and the City Commission. Since the Lexington–Fayette County merger, other cities and their counties have contemplated merger, some even coming to votes, but the opposition of the county judge and county officials would defeat those efforts. Stephens, however, had higher ambitions and did not feel a need to defend the county judge's position. Stephens would be elected attorney general, a justice on the Kentucky Supreme Court and eventually chief justice. The organization of the pro-merger campaign began in the summer and involved hundreds of people. By the end of the voting, over 69 percent voted in favor. Merger was scheduled to take effect on January 1, 1974.

A lawsuit was filed challenging the legality of the process. In September 1973, with the clock running down, the Fayette Circuit Court ruled in favor of the merger plan, but an appeal was taken to the Court of Appeals, at the time the highest state court. In the fall, with one eye on the advancing

Foster Pettit, William Hoskins, Richard Vimont, Dr. J. Farah Van Meter and Scott Yellman filing to run for mayor and city commission. *The University of Kentucky, courtesy of the John C. Watt Lexington–Herald Leader Photograph Collection.*

calendar, briefs were filed and arguments heard. Finally, on December 29, 1973, the court upheld the judgment of the Fayette Circuit Court.

Two days later, the City of Lexington legally disappeared and the Lexington–Fayette County Urban Government was born. One study has determined that, of 105 referenda between 1902 and 2010 on proposed mergers, only 27 succeeded. Lexington's merger was the first in Kentucky. By one measure, it was the twentieth city-county consolidation in the country, but of those put to a popular vote, it was only the twelfth.

Not all of the drama was over the merger itself. The election for the first mayor of the merged government (or the next mayor if the merger vote failed) was hotly contested between incumbent Foster Pettit and challenger James G. Amato. May 1973 saw the first primaries for the Urban County Council as well, with over one hundred candidates standing for fifteen seats. In November, former county judge and representative Bart Peak was elected as an Urban County councilman representing the Fifth Council District.

The election results on November 7 showed Amato had won by a mere 112 votes. A week later, Pettit sued contesting the result, centering his attack particularly on Aylesford precinct near the university, which reported heavily for Amato but Pettit thought he should have won. A court-supervised inspection of the voting machines revealed that, in fact, a vote for Pettit registered for Amato and vice versa. As Pettit described in his book on the election, the turning point was a spider's web across the seam of an access panel, a web the spider would have spun well before the election, thus proving there had been no tampering with the machine. On December 6, the Fayette Circuit Court declared Pettit the victor.

One unanticipated effect of merger was the diminution of the influence of political parties in Lexington. While the city government had been nonpartisan before the merger, county officials were elected on a party basis. As a consequence, a change in the party affiliation of the county judge could mean the loss of jobs by members of the opposite party and the hiring of new people—the old practice of patronage politics. The merged government was entirely nonpartisan, and the roles of the remnants of the county (which could not be eliminated entirely without a state constitutional amendment) were reduced. The influence of the Democratic and Republican Parties, so great at times past in Lexington's history, waned. Candidates for and incumbents in state senate and representative offices began to build their campaigns on personal connections with voters, no longer willing or able to rely upon party machinery to win.

Mayor Pettit, in his inaugural address on New Year's Day, 1974, said: "Today is the first official day of this new experiment in local government. It is very difficult for anyone who is contemporaneous with an event to fully appreciate its significance." In a 2012 interview, Pettit looked back and concluded: "It is impossible to overstate the significance of merger for Lexington." It is beyond the scope of this work to detail the reasons why merger was critical and how it has been successful, but a study of Pettit's personal file on merger, which he generously made available, clearly establishes his point.

As if changing the structure of government were not enough, though, the structure of Lexington's court system also changed in the 1970s, twice.

In 1970, while the Circuit Court system, which heard felonies and major civil actions, was functioning well, it was clear the lower court system was fragmented and inefficient. Lexington had three Magistrate's Courts, a Police Court, a Quarterly Court and a County Court. Prior to 1972, the Police Court was upgraded to a Municipal Court and a Domestic Relations Division was created.

The charter of the merged government abolished the Municipal Court and consolidated the other courts into two, a Quarterly Court and a County

Court, with the magistrates retaining only limited jurisdiction. In 1974, the Quarterly Court had six divisions: criminal, traffic, juvenile, civil, domestic relations and jury trials.

The prior inefficiencies of the lower court system, however, were common to all of Kentucky, and the laws creating many of the lower courts did not require the judges or presiding magistrates to even have law degrees. An omnibus restructuring of Kentucky's courts was presented as a constitutional amendment and adopted in 1975. While the amendment created a new Supreme Court of Kentucky in place "above" the Court of Appeals, it also abolished all of the old lower courts, including those in Lexington, and put in place a new District Court, and the division of jurisdiction between the District and Circuit Courts was clarified. Many of the reforms, policies and procedures developed by Lexington for its revised lower court system were adopted and implemented statewide in the new District Court system as the judicial amendment took effect in 1978.

In 1940, Lexington was an agriculturally focused town of roughly 79,000 people, with downtown businesses lining Main Street and warehouses flanking the railroad tracks running parallel to Main. By 1980, the tracks and warehouses were gone and the population had grown to almost 205,000, a 259 percent increase. The effects cannot be overstated and would be the driving factor in growth, and debate about growth, for the next decades.

Beginning in the 1970s and continuing through the 1980s, the community was remade. Perhaps the best way to illustrate the changes is to just list them:

1975 Rupp Arena and the Civic Center open with controversy over demolition of more than 130 houses for the parking lots between High and Maxwell; the University of Kentucky boasts a record enrollment of 21,488; construction begins on Kincaid Towers (now the Central Bank building); and Lexington acquires federal land for Master Station Park.

1978 The Kentucky Horse Park is established; Good Samaritan Hospital announces a new $9 million, 298-bed addition; and a joint city/state office building is proposed for the east end of downtown.

1979 Mayor James G. Amato, elected in the prior year, initiates reversable lanes on Nicholasville Road and proposes the South Broadway overpass to remove the last railroad track blockage of a major road; Fasig Tipton breaks ground for a new Thoroughbred horse sales pavilion on Newtown Pike.

1980 The first cable television franchise is awarded and channel choices go from four to thirty-six; demolition of the Purcell Block (named for the large former department store, which dominated the block) continues to provide space for another hotel, parking garage and office building; approximately $50 million in highway projects, from new interstate interchanges to widening Versailles Road to replacing downtown viaducts, are underway.

1981 The tobacco markets and warehouses on South Broadway process over 90 million pounds of tobacco, selling for over $164 million; Keeneland sets a Thoroughbred horse sales record topping $300 million, and the following year, Standardbred horse sales exceed $31 million; a $3 million computerized traffic control system is installed; the old Phoenix Hotel, closed for several years, is demolished to make way for a proposed fifty-story World Coal Center; Marriott Resort at Griffin Gate opens; and, in a significant development that would add beauty to downtown for years, sixty-one individuals pledge $10,000 each to establish the Triangle Foundation Inc., whose first project would be converting a gravel parking lot into Triangle Park.

1982 The mounted Horse Patrol unit is introduced downtown; Second National Bank opens its building on the east end at Main and Deweese; and the Hilton Hotel and World Trade Center open.

Between 1980 and 1987, Donald and Dudley Webb, controversial at times, especially with the historic preservation community, alone or with partners build fourteen buildings downtown, including the Hilton and World Trade Center, Victorian Square, Festival Market, the Woodlands condominiums, the chamber of commerce building and the Lexington Financial Center.

With downtown hemmed in between the two universities north and south and residential historic districts at all other compass points, growth necessarily leaps over large residential areas to build office parks along and leading to New Circle Road. Humana Hospital opens a major medical complex on Richmond Road outside of Man-O-War (now St. Joseph Hospital East); Executive Park and Charter Ridge Hospital open; and the Webbs, again, contribute some eighteen suburban office buildings, complexes and shopping centers, including Lexington Green, Corporate Plaza and related buildings, Regency Business Center, Hilton Suites, Tates Creek Center and Perimeter Center Office Park.

1984 The state commits $7.5 million to the construction of Central Park Plaza, which, together with Wallace Wilkinson's contribution, would result in the new main Public Library, Park Plaza apartments and associated garage and Phoenix Park on the site of the former hotel and adjacent land.

1985 Lakepoint East, Fortune Business Center and Chevy Chase Plaza are under development, and for the first time, Lexington and Rupp Arena host the NCAA basketball tournament Final Four games. While not a Lexington event, Toyota announces it will build in Scott County, which does have an effect in Fayette County, as residents will work there and suppliers will be based here.

1987 Planners identify two possible locations for a new regional shopping center: Coldstream Farm on Newtown Pike, owned by the University of Kentucky, and Hamburg Farm on Winchester Road, owned by the Madden family. By year end, the university withdraws Coldstream from consideration, paving the way for the eventual approval and construction of Hamburg Place Mall and adjacent office and residential developments.

1989 IBM reaches its peak of employment, with over 5,700 employees and selling over four million typewriters this year, announcing it will begin producing a new product, a laser printer, in Lexington; and the Urban County Government buys the Kentucky Theater, promising its restoration.

1990 The owners of Fayette Mall win a Kentucky Supreme Court case that orders the rezoning of 23.8 acres at the mall's southern end, allowing an additional 270,000 square feet of shopping space to be constructed; the city adopts the South Broadway Corridor Plan to guide redevelopment of the tobacco warehouse district; and, in September, a 21-acre development at South Broadway and Virginia Avenue is approved as the first such under the new plan.

It is amazing what removing a few railroad tracks and merging a city and a county government can lead to.

New buildings were not the only events in Lexington during this period. Foster Pettit decided not to seek another term as mayor, and attorney Jim Amato, his former opponent, was elected in 1978. Almost immediately, city finances became tight as a lawsuit challenging some property taxes was lost, resulting in a $2.3 million decrease in revenue. Amato proposed a tax increase to make up the difference, but it was rejected by the Urban County

Council. This loss of revenue, coupled with a tougher budget situation in Frankfort, lead to cancelation of the proposed city/state office building on the block east of the Esplanade. Fortunately, the city had an option on the former Kentucky Central Life Insurance building, which would become the new "city hall," prosaically named the Lexington–Fayette Urban County Government Center.

Amato's administration would be characterized by a focus on confronting and fixing transportation issues. He initiated reversable traffic lanes on Nicholasville Road and considered the same for other major arterial roads. Amato pushed for a solution to the last major railroad crossing on South Broadway. The plan approved was a redesign of the street and construction of a railroad overpass; in the process, several popular college bars, notably the popular 803 South and the Upstart Crow, and two strip clubs, were eliminated. Changes to the zoning ordinance removed "gentlemen's clubs" from downtown.

Amato also initiated creation of the Lexington Economic Development Commission. As his term neared completion, Amato enjoyed what the newspaper reported as an 82 percent approval rating, and no one seemed interested in challenging him for a second term. It was a surprise when Amato announced he would not run.

In 1982, District Court judge Scotty Baesler, of Athens in rural Fayette County, was elected mayor to succeed Amato, making Baesler the only non-Lexington resident ever to hold the job.

The Thoroughbred horse industry was rocked in 1984 by the sudden appearance of equine viral arteritis, a disease that can cause mares to abort. Mandatory blood testing of all stallions before the 1985 breeding season was implemented. Three European countries, the source of many buyers, imposed a ban on horses shipped from the United States, a ban lifted only a week before the summer yearling sales. Fortunately, vaccines were available from the University of Kentucky, which had stockpiled the vaccines following an outbreak among Standardbred horses in 1982. By year's end, there were no reported fatalities and no reported abortions.

The following year was a year for bank mergers. Citizens Union was sold to Bank One of Columbus, Ohio, making it the first Lexington bank controlled by an out-of-state entity. First Kentucky National, from Louisville, acquired and merged the Second National Bank and the Bank of Commerce. First Security National Bank & Trust Company, itself the product of prior mergers among Lexington banks, acquired three smaller banks to become the fourth-largest commercial bank in the state.

In February 1986, former mayor Jim Amato opened a new restaurant bearing his name, and in November the voters approved the sale of alcoholic beverages on Sunday, long a goal of the hotel and convention sector. In 1989, Mayor Baesler easily won an unprecedented third term. The following year, a project spearheaded by Baesler, the construction of a major cultural complex on what was known as the Ben Snyder Block (named after the former department store located midblock), took a major step forward when the Urban County Council approved acceptance of $18.5 million from the state to acquire land and build the center. It was planned to have at least two theaters for live performances, smaller practice and rehearsal rooms, a museum and related areas.

Baesler noted in his 1991 "State of the Merged Government" address that, despite a national recession, Lexington's tax revenues grew at an 8 percent rate during the last two quarters and that nearly two-thirds of Kentucky's population growth in the prior ten years had been in Lexington. Baesler, himself, was preparing for a race for governor. He would lose to Woodford County horseman Brereton Jones.

While Baesler was reporting good news for Lexington as a whole, trouble was beginning in a leading Lexington company. Kentucky Central Life Insurance Co., the second-largest insurance company in Kentucky, experienced a $38.8 million loss in the last nine months of 1991, the largest in its eighty-nine years of operations. The primary cause was excessive overdue loans and foreclosed real estate. Several prominent developers and locally prominent individuals also received high loans at under market rates. The financial irregularities, which involved more than thirty different borrowers, led to total losses of over $141 million over several years. On February 12, 1993, the Kentucky Department of Insurance seized Kentucky Central. Its assets, including the insurance business, banks, television and radio stations and real estate holdings were sold off over the next two years.

By this time, however, Baesler had been elected to the U.S. Congress representing central Kentucky, and Vice Mayor Pam Miller became the first woman mayor of Lexington. Baesler left office having served as mayor longer than any other individual in the history of the merged government and second longest in the history of Lexington.

One of Mayor Miller's early, and pleasant, duties was to receive the deed to twenty acres around McConnell Springs, the founding site of Lexington, in a ceremony on November 22, 1993. The city proposed to clean up the area, long a waste dump, while a citizens group, Friends of McConnell Springs, began raising donations to build a visitor's center and provide parking and other features. As councilwoman and future vice mayor Isabel Yates, a leader of the preservation effort, said at the event, "This is a project that is just plain right."

Not far away, in the heart of downtown, another small tract of land was causing a much bigger problem. In 1991, the state bought several buildings on the northeast corner of Limestone and Main comprising roughly two acres for $9 million, with the agreement of the city to build a $14 million cultural center on the property. Mayor Miller had to cancel the project, as the city could not afford it—but the state wanted its money back. Miller appointed a committee chaired by former mayor Foster Pettit to make a recommendation, but the only proposal generated was for a new "justice center." However, that would require state funding, and none was approved.

Miller attempted to negotiate some solution with Governor Brereton Jones, but in the spring of 1995, she was forced to concede that Jones had the upper hand and unhappily accepted dictated terms of repayment. The city would have to pay the state $16.9 million over sixteen years. No one, except the governor, was pleased. Eventually, the commonwealth filed suit against the Urban County to collect the money.

However, a new governor, Paul Patton, was elected. Miller was able to quickly work out a solution with him, and they announced it in a joint news conference on the courthouse steps on April 25, 1995. As the *Herald Leader* reported, it took three governors, two mayors, three citizens' study committees, a state audit and a lawsuit to resolve the matter. The litigation was dropped, the city committed to spend $15 million on cultural projects—a downtown arts center, restoration of the State and Lyric Theaters, a grant to the Lexington Children's Theater—and fund a basketball museum. The state would take most of the land for what were ultimately two new courthouses. When the old courthouse was vacated, the city would renovate it for the Lexington History Museum, the creation of which was part of the agreement. Shortly afterwards the mayor's office called attorneys Steve Amato, son of the former mayor, and Foster Ockerman Jr. and directed them to establish the museum.

Business was good in Lexington; employers struggled to hire and retain good employees, who often left for better jobs. Joseph Beth Booksellers became one of the largest independent bookstores when it moved into the forty-seven-thousand-square-foot central area of Lexington Green. In July 1996, the Madden family announced the first occupants of space in their new regional shopping center, Target department store and a twenty-screen theater. Their plans for a one-million-square-foot enclosed mall had been changed into clustered store groups. Northpark Theater, however, closed.

19

GROWTH VERSUS NO GROWTH

The early years of the Miller administration were characterized by debate over growth. Popular bumper stickers concisely stated the competing cases: "Growth is Good" vs. "Growth Destroys Bluegrass Forever." In 1994, the Greenspace Plan was adopted as a part of the Comprehensive Plan, and arguments for and against expanding the urban service boundary were made. The 1996 Comprehensive Plan included three designated expansion areas with particular rules governing the development of each.

The following year, the minimum-size tract outside the boundary was increased from ten to forty acres to better preserve the rural character of the county. Finally, major preservation efforts were capped with the adoption in 2001 of the Purchase of Development Rights Program, funded initially by the Urban Council with $40 million. The program assesses rural property submitted by owners on a variety of aspects ranging from quality of soil to the presence of wetlands and, based on the point totals, offers to buy the right to development a property from its owner. If the owner sells and subjects the property to the restrictions of the program, the ability to develop the land as other than farmland is gone. The goal was to preserve 50,000 Fayette County acres. By the beginning of 2021, 277 farms containing over 30,550 acres had been protected with conservation easements and the program was more than halfway to the goal.

Over three years of contentious meetings, public and private, Miller managed to forge a compromise, if not a consensus. Attorney Bill Lear, who

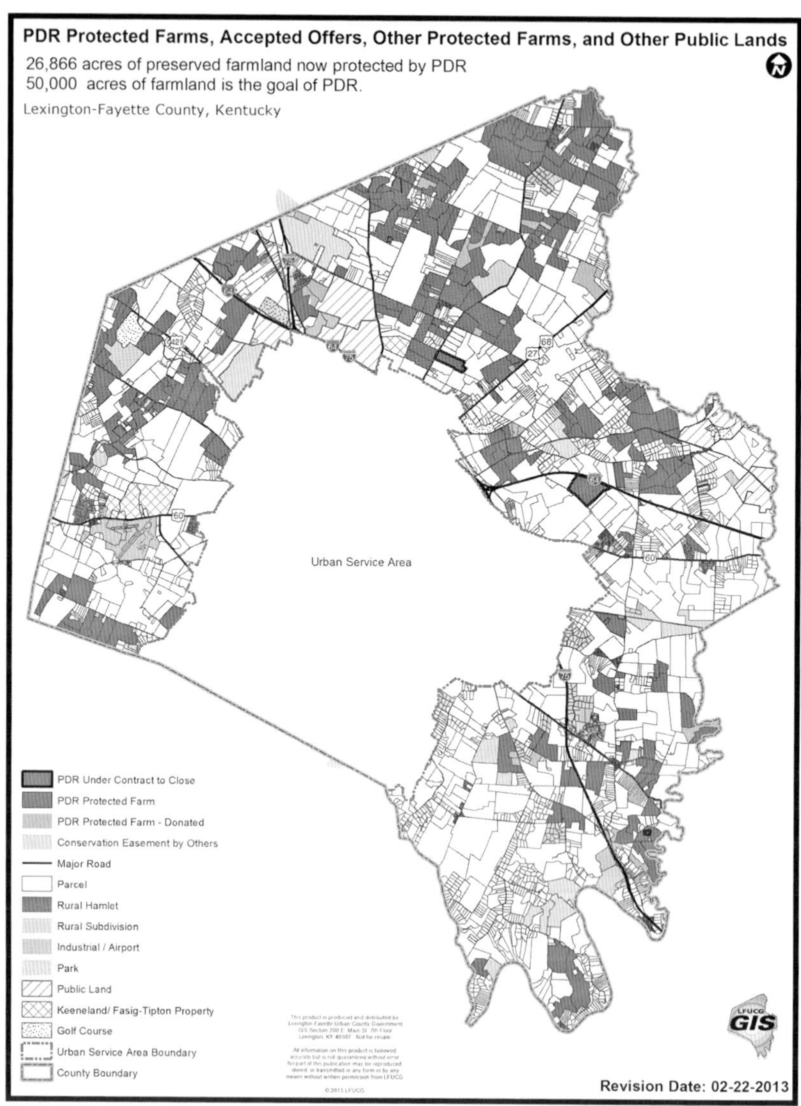

Map of preserved farmland. *Lexington–Fayette Urban County Government.*

frequently represented developers, summarized Miller's accomplishment this way: "She was able to accomplish the number one item on the preservationists' agenda and the number one item on the developers' agenda."

The interface of urban and rural land uses was not the only focus of the Miller administration. Miller formed a committee in 1999 to focus on downtown redevelopment and directed the creation of the nonprofit Lexington Downtown Development Authority Inc. to provide assistance for downtown projects. Lexington's population had grown to over 260,000.

Lexington has not been a hospitable environment for professional sports teams. In this period, attempts were made to establish an ice hockey team (twice) and indoor arena football. But in 2001, Alan Stein succeeded where the others did not and started the Lexington Legends minor league baseball team, playing in a new ballpark on North Broadway.

As Mayor Miller's second full term drew to a close in 2002, the next major community issue was developing. A German-based multinational multi-utility whose name was abbreviated RWE AG proposed to purchase the parent company of Kentucky American Water Co., which held the Lexington water franchise. Former governor Edward T. "Ned" Breathitt was opposed to the sale and began a citizen effort to persuade the Urban County to purchase the utility. He incorporated Bluegrass FLOW (For Local Ownership of Water) Inc. and organized leading citizens in the effort. Among the members of the initial board of directors were former mayor Foster Pettit, attorney Foster Ockerman, businessmen Warren Rosenthal, Thomas Dupree, Bill Sturgill and Joe Graves, horseman John Gaines, historian Dr. Thomas Clark, former newspaper editor Don Mills, former UK basketball coach Joe B. Hall and former Ford Motor Co. official John Burkhardt. Attorney Foster Ockerman Jr. became counsel to the new nonprofit. FLOW, as it came to be called, immediately moved to intervene before the Public Service Commission to oppose the sale; the motion was granted over the opposition of the water company. The Urban Council, meanwhile, voted to ask the PSC to put meaningful conditions on any sale to RWE while it explored its options to purchase the company.

The Urban County Council hired an attorney with condemnation experience to advise it and in July advertised for a valuation consultant to tell it how much the utility was worth. The water company stated it was not for sale.

The mayor's race to succeed Miller was particularly contentious and, for the first time, partisan, with the Republican Party in Fayette openly supporting Scott Crosbie, putting the Democratic Party in a similar posture

A "Let us Vote" petition drive organizing meeting. *Foster Ockerman, Jr.*

for former vice mayor Teresa Isaac, despite the fact that under the Urban County Charter, the race was nonpartisan. Isaac supported local ownership of the water company. Isaac won the election. While her election was not taken as a statement on ownership of the water company, it was generally accepted as a statement that the political parties should not be active in Urban County races.

During the campaign, Lexington's new courthouses were dedicated as the Robert F. Stephens Courthouses, in honor of Fayette County's last premerger county judge and eventual chief justice of the Kentucky Supreme Court.

Mayor Isaac had hardly assumed office when the city was struck by a major winter ice storm in February 2003. Almost all of Lexington and surrounding areas lost electric power, in some places for over a week. Broken limbs and downed trees and power lines littered the community, blocking many roads. After the thaw, the clean-up took weeks.

Isaac won praise for her crisis management, spending hours in her office leading her commissioners and holding frequent press conferences. This same leadership style served her again when a Black robbery suspect was fatally shot by a white policeman. Isaac drove to the scene in the early morning hours, rousing first her staff and then community leaders to share information and defuse a potential crisis.

Her relationship with the council, however, soured, and she had frequent exchanges with Vice Mayor Mike Scanlon, who also opposed local ownership of the water company.

The "water war," as it came to be known, lasted five years and involved challenges from FLOW in circuit court and before the PSC. The Urban County filed a condemnation suit in Fayette Circuit Court in the summer of 2003 to acquire the company by eminent domain. Breathitt died unexpectedly in October 2003. Pettit took over leadership of FLOW, and Foster Ockerman Jr. became the public spokesperson for the organization. He made many public and media appearances arguing the case for local ownership, frequently debating opponents thereof, including Kentucky American attorney Bill Lear and businessman Warren Rogers, who led a citizens group opposing ownership. On October 18, 2006, radio station WVLK sponsored and broadcast live a spirited debate before a packed crowd in the theater of the downtown branch of the public library between Ockerman and Vice Mayor Scanlon.

Council elections in 2004 changed enough members on the council to reverse the majority for local ownership, and the new council began to unwind the legal action. The reaction of the pro-ownership faction was to begin a petition to put the issue on the ballot for a referendum, and Let Us Vote Lexington Inc. was formed, led by attorney Jane Graham. Its only cause was a public vote, and it consequently attracted individuals on both sides of the issue to collect and sign petitions. Though it needed fewer than nineteen thousand valid signatures to succeed, the petition drive resulted in over twenty-three thousand signatures.

The issue would head to a public vote, but the next issue was when. No regular election was scheduled for November 2005. The water company sued to stop a vote at that time, saying an election had to be scheduled before a referendum could be added to the ballot. Ultimately, the Kentucky Supreme Court agreed and ordered the referendum vote to take place in November 2006.

That put the referendum on the same ballot as the mayoral and council races, and local ownership became a campaign issue. Some thought it might have passed as a stand-alone issue in 2005, but the delay afforded the utility time to mount a massive "vote no" advertising campaign, far outspending the resources available to FLOW.

Isaac still supported local ownership. Her challenger, attorney Jim Newberry, was publicly neutral and willing to obey the vote result, but heavily supported by water company supporters. Newberry won with almost two-thirds of the vote, carrying 220 of 250 precincts. Jim Gray was elected as vice mayor.

The referendum lost by 47,951 to 30,920 votes. Breathitt wrote an opinion essay published in the newspaper on February 10, 2002, advocating local ownership, and the water company took that date on its website to count the days of the "attempted takeover." The referendum was defeated on day 1,731.

Newberry's soft-spoken manner and quiet style was a studied contrast to Isaac, and with Gray's demeanor, several degrees cooler than Scanlon's, council meetings were calmer events.

20

MODERN LEXINGTON

Lexington had a population of almost 300,000 when Jim Gray was elected mayor in November 2010, defeating the incumbent Newberry with 53 percent of the vote. Notable, and reflective of Lexington's generally progressive character, Gray was the first openly gay mayor in Kentucky.

Faced with a $9 million deficit in the urban county budget for fiscal year 2011 and a projected shortfall of $27 million in fiscal 2012, Gray made massive and ultimately successful efforts to balance the budget, becoming the first mayor to successfully use the veto power over financial matters. Gray also intentionally sought a more open appearance in government and symbolized that by moving the mayor's office out of twelfth-floor seclusion into the ballroom of the city building on the first floor, with his desk in the center surrounded by his staff.

One of the problems Gray inherited was a $296 million underfunded police and fire pension system. After months of negotiations with public safety representatives, a deal was reached in early 2013 to increase city funding, with increased contributions by members and other modifications. The solution required the approval of the General Assembly, which came in the spring.

Gray also brought an innovative approach to other issues, showing a willingness if not a determination to think outside the box. He brought in an international architect to guide a citizens task force he appointed to a new vision for Rupp Arena, the Civic Center and what is called the Rupp

Mayor Jim Gray being sworn into office. © *The University of Kentucky, courtesy of the John C. Watt Lexington–Herald Leader Photograph Collection.*

Former mayors Isaac, Miller, Baesler, Amato and Pettit at Mayor Gray's ceremony, 2008. © *The University of Kentucky, courtesy of the John C. Watt Lexington–Herald Leader Photograph Collection.*

Arena Arts and Entertainment District. He initiated discussions with the owners of a block of downtown property in an effort to improve on the design for the buildings to be built there. He joined with new Louisville mayor Greg Fisher in a new initiative to promote economic development between the two cities.

The historic 1899 Old Courthouse, home to the Lexington History Museum, was closed to the public on July 13, 2012, when unacceptably dangerous levels of lead dust were discovered in the building. The museum was forced to cease operations in the building and, with the help of the public library and other venues, began moving some of its exhibits to other places, concentrating on developing mobile programming while the Old Courthouse was restored. In December 2012, Gray gave approval to the Downtown Development Authority and the Courthouse Square Foundation Inc., chaired by former city CAO Frank Mattone, with Foster Ockerman Jr. as president, to begin developing a plan for restoring the Old Courthouse to its original design, a process that could take several years.

Across the street from the Old Courthouse, 21C Museum Hotels acquired the historic First National Bank building with plans to convert it into a boutique hotel and art museum. The imminent arrival of a 21C Hotel will cap a renaissance of the old town square, now in the midst of several new or relocated restaurants and with community gathering space under the new pavilion erected on a redesigned and developed Cheapside Park, which occasioned the relocation of the statute of Breckinridge from the center of the park facing the courthouse to the Main Street frontage.

The churches of Lexington continued to thrive and, for some congregations, expand. Most notable was the Southland Christian Church megachurch with a 115-acre site south of Lexington and over seven thousand in attendance each week. Immanuel Baptist served over four thousand members on its 22-acre campus. The mainline churches downtown maintain a steady membership while others have adopted a multicampus approach to growth. Southland Christian opened its third campus at the former Lexington Mall at the start of 2013, and First United Methodist Church, with campuses downtown and on Todds Road, opened a third campus the same year.

As this history draws a line in time, Lexington is returning to its roots as a historic center for education, medicine, agriculture and horses.

As it has from the earliest days, education continues to play a major role in Lexington.

Having completed a major expansion of its medical center facilities, in 2013 the University of Kentucky received approval from the General

Assembly to proceed with $250 million in construction projects, including a new science building, expansion of the business college and renovations to Commonwealth Stadium. It contracted with a private company to build a new six-hundred-bed dormitory and made plans to add or replace nine thousand dorm beds on campus. In 2021, the iconic Kirwin and Blanding residential towers were torn down. The housing boom is not only on campus. At least ten privately owned residential complexes have been constructed on South Broadway, replacing the many tobacco warehouses, potentially housing over two thousand students. One complex has a bridge over the railroad tracks connecting to the UK campus.

Yet to be seen is what the effects of more housing on campus, and more housing west of campus, will have on the residential blocks on the fringes of campus where many former single-family residences were divided into rooming houses and apartments for students.

Transylvania University was also expanding, having bought land near its downtown campus for new athletics facilities on ten acres on Fourth Street, including a new grandstand and a new building for coaches' offices, a training room and a locker room.

Nearby, the Bluegrass Community and Technical College took ownership of the grounds of the former Eastern State Hospital and approved a twenty-year plan for the forty-eight-acre site. Some buildings will be restored and more than fourteen new buildings constructed over time. It was made possible by an innovative arrangement with UK and Eastern State Hospital whereby Eastern State builds a new facility on UK's Coldstream Farm research campus, BCTC gets the Eastern State property and UK will get BCTC's former facilities on Cooper Drive. In 2013, BCTC announced the acquisition of an additional twelve acres.

Combined, the three institutions educate over forty-five thousand students each year.

Growth was not only at the higher education level. Fayette County public schools have an enrollment of over forty thousand students, and the number is increasing. To add to the then thirty elementary, twelve middle and five high schools, plus four alternative and technical high schools, the facilities plan called for a new high school, a new middle school and two new elementary schools.

Lexington continued to expand its medical facilities. Not only did UK construct a $592 million hospital bed tower at the Medical Center, but it also acquired the former Good Samaritan Hospital at Limestone and Maxwell. Central Baptist Hospital was in the midst of a $200 million renovation and expansion for a new underground parking garage, oncology center and women's center. When complete, the facility, renamed Baptist Health Lexington, will have 383 private beds. It also owned 129 acres in the Hamburg area east of the interstate for future use. Baptist has also opened small satellite facilities in the suburbs for outpatient services.

The Shriners Hospital for Children built a new facility across Limestone Street from the University of Kentucky medical complex.

The Fayette County Farm Bureau sponsored a project by the UK College of Agriculture to study the economic impact of agriculture, including not only traditional elements like farms but also the broader impact of businesses, professions and trades that rely upon, work for or service what the report called the "Ag Cluster." The report was published in January 2013. The Ag Cluster, it found, generated about $2.4 billion in output, $66 million in taxes and $47 million in occupational licenses fees for Fayette County.

Over 18,000 jobs, roughly one in nine, in Fayette County are directly or indirectly associated with agriculture, which in Kentucky includes horses. In 2011, the Lexington Junior League held its 75th annual charity horse show and honored the only person to have both competed in a show and served as horse show chair, Joyce H. Ockerman, daughter of the first horse show manager, Jeff Harris. Keeneland's total sales volume for 2012 was over $410 million. The Kentucky Horse Park hosted three of the top twenty-five horse shows as ranked by the North American Riders Group, the only North American site to have more than one. The highest ranked was the Alltech National Horse Show, which debuted in Lexington for the first time in 2011 for its 128th competition. Begun in Madison Square Garden in 1883, it is the oldest indoor horse show in the country. The Horse Park was the site in 2010 of the FEI World Equestrian Games, the first time championships in all eight disciplines were held at one location. Held for the first time outside of Europe, this edition featured 632 riders and 752 horses from 58 countries competing before over 500,000 attendees over sixteen days. There were more than three hundred hours of international television broadcasts of the Games.

Lexington is not only returning to its roots, it is returning to its waters as well. On the banks of Town Branch of the Elkhorn River, whose stream bed was successively the route of commerce for boats, mills and distilleries, rail and automobile, Mayor Gray announced plans in 2013 to resurrect elements of Town Branch along the Vine Street corridor and reveal and improve the stream west of Rupp Arena. He noted that Lexington was one of the largest cities in the United States not to be on a major lake or river and, following the example of a city in South Korea that "day lighted" a river it had previously paved over, revealed plans to revive the course of Town Branch from near its headwater close to Midland Avenue and Winchester Road, down Midland and Vine Streets to the Civic Center. At the west end of the Civic Center/Rupp Arena complex, the Branch would reemerge to flow through a new Town Branch Park to exit downtown through the new Distillery District, a former warehouse area newly reinvented with shops, bars and restaurants.

Finally, Gray pushed through action on the renovation of the Civic Center and Rupp Arena buildings after "years of studies." By the end of his two terms as mayor, he noted he had learned that "planning is a big piece of a project."

The culmination of the resolution of the "growth vs. no growth" debate was a "grow up, not out" policy shift. The planning process began to emphasize putting vacant or underdeveloped parcels of land to a higher use. There was no bigger example of this than the downtown block bounded by Limestone, Vine, Upper and Main Streets, right in the heart of the city. Although the block was majority asphalt, when the Webb Companies acquired control of the block and razed the remaining buildings, there was an outcry from some preservationists. Economic conditions prevented an immediate redevelopment of the block, and for three years it became a grassy semipark. However, construction eventually began on a JW Marriott Hotel, a Renaissance Hotel, an office tower and a steak house restaurant with an underground garage. The complex opened in the fall of 2019.

In November 2018, Vice Mayor Linda Gorton, the Urban Council's longest serving member, was elected as the third female mayor of Lexington with 63 percent of the vote. Almost immediately, it was revealed that the finances of the government were in rough shape again, and she had to initiate belt-tightening measures. Cuts in city funds to many agencies and arts and cultural groups were made. Just when Gorton began to get her hands around finances, the COVID virus pandemic hit Lexington and the country in March 2020. Lexington's budget is heavily dependent on payroll taxes, and the large numbers of businesses that had to close, with the dismissal of employees, put a further financial burden on the government.

At this writing in February 2021, the supply of vaccines nationally and locally is slowing increasing. Former mayor Gray, who was once president of a major construction company, was named secretary of transportation just before a major fire severely damaged the bridge connecting Kentucky to Cincinnati. Just as Secretary Gray completed supervision of the repair and reopening of the bridge, he was tapped by Governor Andy Beshear to oversee vaccine distribution in Kentucky.

Testing sites and, shortly, vaccination sites gradually increased across the community, and as spring approached, Lexington was eager to reopen in-person school classes, business and other activity.

On a positive note, Mayor Gorton appointed the Mayor's Commission for Racial Justice & Equality, which delivered its report and recommendations to the Mayor in October 2020. The Commission was composed of judges, educators, social workers, men and women from the business community, community activists, faith leaders, representatives from the law enforcement services and elected leaders. The commission formed itself into five committees to address different issues. The mayor is now engaged in putting into place recommendations by the commission.

21

A RETROSPECTIVE

It can be difficult to encapsule almost two and a half centuries of a community, but if there is a common thread, it is that almost every time Lexington was about to make a major misstep, someone stood up with a better idea.

Robert Todd started the first passenger railroad in the United States in the 1830s.

Maria Gratz, wife of Benjamin Gratz, opened a major orphanage to take care of those who lost their parents to the cholera epidemic of 1833.

Progressive leaders in the late nineteenth century reformed city government and put an end to corrupt "boss" rule.

Mayor Hogan Yancey refused to allow the Ku Klux Klan to march, rally and recruit in Lexington, with the result that a KKK chapter was never formed in Lexington.

In a post–World War II economic boom, business leaders made the decision not to recruit "smokestack" industry and, instead, bought land and developed an office park that eventually attracted major companies like IBM.

To preserve horse farms and agricultural land surrounding the city proper, the Urban Service Boundary—the first of its kind in the nation—was established.

Mayor Foster Pettit rejected allowing an interstate to be run through the middle of downtown, led the political fight to merge the city and county and then guided the new government onto its initial path.

When the Black Lives Matter movement erupted across the county with violent demonstrations, Lexington had a coterie of Black leaders who helped moderate conversations, resulting in peaceful demonstrations and marches in Lexington. In modern times, Lexington has had two Black chiefs of police, two Black presidents of the United Way of the Bluegrass and a Black newspaper publisher.

Finally, Lexington elected a registered nurse in Mayor Linda Gorton, just before a pandemic hit, who had the knowledge and training to understand what was occurring.

This is not to say there have not been missteps and mistakes, nor that national events like depressions and the Civil War did not overcome local leadership, but surveying Lexington's history as a whole, it has exhibited a progressive attitude open to new ideas and civic improvement not every community can boast.

Appendix A

MAYORS OF LEXINGTON

1832	Charlton Hunt
1835	James E. Davis
1837	James G. McKinney
1839	Charles H. Wickliffe
1841	Daniel Bradford
1842	James Logue
1846	Thomas Ross
1847	John Henry
1848	George Payne Jouett
1849	Orlando F. Payne
1851	Edward W. Dowden
1854	Thomas Hart Pindell
1855	William Swift
1859	Thomas B. Monroe Jr.
1860	Benjamin F. Graves
1862	Caleb Thompson Worley
1863	Joseph Wingate, Jr.
1866	David W. Standeford
1867	Jerry T. Frazer
1868	Joseph G. Chinn
1869	Jerry T. Frazer
1880	Claudius M. Johnson Jr.
1888	Charles W. Foushee
1892	J. Hull Davidson
1894	Henry T. Duncan
1896	Joseph Bullock Simrall
1900	Henry T. Duncan
1904	Thomas A. Combs
1907	R. B. Waddy
1908	John Skain
1912	J. Ernest Cassidy
1916	James C. Rogers
1919	William H. McCorkle
1920	Thomas Clark Bradley
1924	Hogan Yancey
1928	James J. O'Brien
1932	William Thomas Congleton
1934	Charles R. Thompson
1935	E. Reed Wilson
1940	T. Ward Havely
1943	R. Mack Oldham
1948	Thomas G. Mooney
1952	Fred Fugazzi
1956	Shelby C. Kinkead
1960	Richard J. Colbert
1964	Fred Fugazzi

1968 Charles Wylie
1972 Foster Pettit
1978 James G. Amato
1982 Scotty Baesler
1993 Pam Miller
2002 Teresa Isaac
2006 Jim Newberry
2010 Jim Gray
2018 Linda Gorton

APPENDIX B
GOVERNMENTS OF LEXINGTON

Lexington has experienced or chosen almost every form of government known except a benevolent dictatorship—and there is an argument Billy "King" Klair was that. Here is the sequence of Lexington's changing governmental structure:

1775	Founded nominally under the English monarchy, although the Revolution had begun.
1780	Articles of Agreement, a citizens compact not unlike the Mayflower Compact, with a five-man "board."
1782	By act of the Virginia legislature, Lexington is chartered as a town with a board of seven trustees who elected their own successors and filled vacancies. About this time, the original boundaries were enlarged to a radius of one mile from the courthouse.
1811	The number of trustees is increased to eleven.
1831	City incorporates with a twelve-member popularly elected city council, which in turn appoints the mayor. The mayor was both the executive and a judge. One of these first councilmen was Robert Todd, father of Mary Todd Lincoln.
1835	The Kentucky Court rules combining executive and judicial functions in one office unconstitutional, and the judicial role is removed from the mayor's authority.
1862–65	Martial law is declared in Lexington and government by a Union general.

1882 Charter is changed to make the mayor elected by popular vote.

1886 Charter is amended to establish a bicameral legislature, with a twelve-member Board of Councilmen and an eight-member Board of Aldermen.

1913 The city commission form is adopted, with a mayor and four commissioners, all elected.

1930 City manager form of government chosen, adding a manager hired by the city council as the chief administrator.

1974 Merger of the city and county to form the Urban County Government with a mayor and fifteen councilmembers, twelve elected from districts and three from the county at large.

Appendix C
SEALS OF THE CITY

Lexington, and now the Urban County, has had four official seals.

The first seal, adopted on October 21, 1800, was simple stamp with the letters "TL" inside a circle, likely referring to the Trustees of Lexington, who governed the town at the beginning. It was used to authenticate official documents.

The second seal was adopted on January 12, 1832, when Lexington was incorporated. It has been described as having a beehive, an argus, a naked arm on the right side, a cornucopia on the left side and a glove over the hive in a riot of symbolism. The original Argus was a hundred-eyed monster of Greek mythology, and the word later meant a watchful guardian. It may have been represented as an eye similar to the eye in the pyramid on the back of a one-dollar bill.

The third seal, adopted on January 26, 1916, was described in the newspaper as "a river scene with crossed arrows and a sheaf of wheat, or something." It may have been a stand of hemp or cane, both more likely in Kentucky than wheat, although after the argus, it is hard to guess at the intent of the symbols.

The fourth and present seal has an interesting origin. In the early 1960s, there was a discussion about a new seal. The mayor, Fred Fugazzi, asked the public for proposals, but when they came in he was disappointed. When he came home the evening before the city council meeting that was to vote on which to adopt, he said so to his wife, Elizabeth Nunn Fugazzi. She was an artist and promptly took out a piece of shirt cardboard and began designing at the kitchen table.

The mayor took her artwork and submitted it anonymously, and it was chosen over the others. Only after the vote did he reveal the identity of the artist. On December 17, 1964, the seal was officially adopted by Ordinance No. 5081. In the center is Old Morrison on the Transylvania campus, representing Lexington's strong connections to education, surmounted by a horseshoe and flanked by tobacco leaves, signaling the importance of those industries. Below the building is the city founding year of 1775. Originally, "City of Lexington" was in the ring around the images at the top and "Commonwealth of Kentucky" around the bottom. The only change since 1964 has been to surround the seal with "Lexington Fayette Urban County Government" and just "Kentucky" at the bottom.

Appendix D

LEXINGTON IN THE U.S. SUPREME COURT

Lexington made an early appearance in a case before the U.S. Supreme Court over a land dispute with the McConnell family, of McConnell Springs fame. It centered on whether the McConnells owned a lot in the middle of the growing town that they used for a tannery or whether the City Trustees could force a removal of the tannery. A tannery, where hides are cleaned of animal flesh and finished into leather, creates horrible odors. While there may have been an advantage to having a tannery inside the walls of Lexington Station while there was an Indian threat, it now was an odorous and undesirable feature—especially as it was next to the spring from which the residents drew water daily.

McConnell v. Trustees of Town of Lexington, 25 U.S. 12 Wheat. 582 582 (1827)

ERROR TO THE COURT OF THE UNITED STATES FOR THE SEVENTH CIRCUIT AND DISTRICT OF KENTUCKY

Syllabus

A question in equity as to the title to a lot of land in the Town of Lexington, Kentucky, reserved as public property and claimed as having been appropriated by the plaintiff's ancestor. Bill dismissed under the circumstances of the case.

MR. CHIEF JUSTICE MARSHALL delivered the opinion of the Court.

This suit was brought in the Court of the United States for the Seventh Circuit and District of Kentucky against the trustees of the Town of

Lexington and others to obtain a conveyance of in and out lots No. 43 in that town or of such other lots in lieu of them as might still remain to be conveyed by the trustees. The whole of out lot No. 43, and a part of the in lot, had been conveyed to other persons who had been in possession for such a length of time as to bar the plaintiff's action. The bill was therefore dismissed by the plaintiff as against those defendants and continued against the trustees.

The Commonwealth of Virginia had, in 1773, by an act commonly called "the land law," reserved 640 acres of land for the benefit of those who had settled in a village or station, that it might be afterwards laid out into lots for a town and divided among such settlers. The inhabitants of Lexington purchased 70 acres adjoining the reserve of 640 acres, and after laying the whole off in lots and streets, petitioned the assembly to establish a town. The legislature, in May, 1782, passed an act vesting the whole 710 acres in trustees who were empowered to make conveyances to those persons who had already settled on the said lots, as also to the purchasers of lots theretofore sold, and to lay off such other parts of the said land as was not then laid off and settled into lots and streets, and to sell or otherwise dispose of the same for the benefit of the inhabitants.

James McConnell was one of the settlers in Lexington and was killed by the Indians in 1782. His brother and heir at law, Alexander McConnell, filed this bill in 1815, and founds his claim on proof that he had in his lifetime erected a tannery on in lot No. 43 on which was a large spring, and on the following order of the board of trustees:

"At a meeting of the board of trustees for the Town of Lexington, September 30, 1782, No. 43 in and out lot granted to James McConnell, to be appraised, and the valuation thereof redound to the heirs of said McConnell, deceased."

The trustees in their answer insist that in lot No. 43 never was granted to James McConnell, but a part of it has always been considered as reserved, on account of a spring upon it, for the use of the inhabitants. They are informed by the old settlers that the privilege of establishing a tannery on that lot was in the year 1781 granted to James McConnell, who did establish one, and that the order of appraisement was intended to cause a valuation of the improvements and of the leather in the tannery, not of the lot itself, and that so much of the entry as applies to the lot itself is a mistake of the clerk. They say that other lots, not these, were granted to McConnell. They also insist on the length of time which has elapsed and on the statute of limitations.

Several certificates from the clerk and extracts from the record books of the trustees are filed as exhibits in the cause. From one of these certificates it appears that on 20 December, 1781, at the first arrangement of in and out lots of the Town of Lexington among the settlers, in lot No. 18, and out lot No. 37 were granted to James McConnell as his donation lots. The out lot appears to have been transferred by John Clarke, whose connection with McConnell is not stated, to Robert Parker, to whose assignee a conveyance was made by the trustees in August, 1785.

An assignment by Alexander McConnell, as heir at law of James, of his title to an out lot in the Town of Lexington, made in May, 1795, is produced, but this assignment neither mentions the number of the lot nor the name of the assignee.

Another certificate from the clerk states that in lot No. 18 was granted on 26 March, 1781, to William Stule, and afterward, on 20 December, 1781, to Benjamin Hayden. It was afterwards, on 1 July, 1783, awarded to James McConnell, and afterwards, on 8 March, 1785, was forfeited. The cause of forfeiture is not mentioned. The presumption is that it must have been on account of the nonperformance of some condition on which the allotment was made.

The entries of the orders made by the trustees seem to be in great confusion. This may be well accounted for by the then situation of that country. Sometime in the year 1784 or 1785, Robert Parker, then clerk of the board of trustees, was ordered to transcribe their old books. Many of their entries were made on small scraps of paper and on backs of old letters. The book then made out is said to be lost. There is, however, a book of records.

The imperfect and confused state of the books has made it necessary to resort to the testimony of witnesses to supply facts which the books do not disclose.

It is very well ascertained that the large spring below which McConnell's tan vats were sunk was enclosed within the stockade, and was used by the inhabitants of the fort generally. It is also in proof that the settlers were each entitled to an in and out lot, and that the trustees frequently allowed those who were dissatisfied with the lots which they drew to exchange them for others not previously granted.

William Stule, who was one of the original trustees, deposes that the lot on which the tan vats were sunk in spring, 1782, was called McConnell's Lot, but he does not recollect any contract between McConnell and the trustees, or any disposition made by them of the lot, until a part of it was given to Bradford, on which to erect a printing office.

Robert Patterson was also one of the original trustees, and was friend and relation of McConnell. He deposes that McConnell was a tanner; the trustees being desirous to attract tradesmen to the station, permitted McConnell to erect a tan yard on the lot in contest about the fall, 1781. That the deponent was authorized by the trustees about the year 1783 or 1784, to clear out and wall up the public spring, for which he was paid by them. That it was called and used as the public spring from the first settlement of the town. He believes McConnell was permitted to use part of the lot as a tannery for the people of the town because it was more convenient, and under cover of the fort. While thus used, it was called McConnell's Tan Yard. He does not know that the trustees intended to make any other grant of the lot than to suffer its use by McConnell.

They fixed a market house on the lot in 1790 or 1791, and then claimed it as their own property. They granted part of it in the year 1787 to John Bradford on condition of his establishing a printing office on it, reserving the public spring and a considerable front on Main and Water Streets, on which they erected buildings which were rented to Bradford. They reserved a number of lots for public use.

John Torrence, William Martin, Samuel Martin, Benjamin Hayden, Joseph Mitchell, Josiah Collins, and Hugh Thompson were among the early settlers of Lexington, and were examined, some of them by the appellant and some by the trustees. They all concur in the declarations that the spring was public, for the use of the people of the fort generally; that it was called the public spring; some that it was called the public spring lot; that McConnell sank vats and constructed a tan yard on it, after which it was called McConnell's Tan Yard, and one witness is inclined to think McConnell's Lot. They all concur, however, in denying having ever heard that the lot was given to McConnell or to any other person. Some say, though they never heard him claim the lot, they have heard him claim the tan yard. Joseph Mitchell swears that McConnell claimed a lot in a different square. Hugh Thomson says that the records of the trustees, which are produced to him at the time his deposition is taken, plainly show that in lot No. 18, and out lot No. 38, were granted to James McConnell. John Parker and Alexander Parker came to Lexington, the one in 1783 and the other in 1784. They were each of them members of the board of trustees, and depose to the universal understanding that the spring lot was reserved for public use and had never been granted to any person until a part of it was granted to Bradford for a printing office. Alexander Parker says that on looking into the record books while a trustee, he saw with surprise the entry under which Alexander McConnell claims, and on making inquiries from Col. Robert Patterson, also a trustee, was informed that the trustees had prevailed on James McConnell to establish a tannery under cover of the fort to tan buffalo hides, and had, after his death, appointed appraisers to value his property. That the entry appears in its present form is the mistake of the clerk who made it. He adds that the records show that in lot No. 18 and out lot No. 38 were granted to James McConnell.

The entry under which the appellant claims lot No. 43 does not purport to grant him that lot, but directs a valuation in terms which import a former grant. No trace of that former grant is, however, found, and the testimony is very strong to prove it was never made. The reasonableness of reserving a public spring for public use, the concurrent opinion of all the settlers that it was so reserved, the universal admission of all that it was never understood that the spring lot was drawn by any person, the early appropriation of it to public purposes, the fact that James McConnell actually claimed a different lot, added to the length of time which has been permitted to elapse without any assertion of title to this lot, are, we think, decisive against the appellant.

There was no error in dismissing the plaintiff's bill, and the decree is *Affirmed with costs.*

INDEX

E

F

G

H

I

J

K

L

M

ABOUT THE AUTHOR

Foster Ockerman Jr., a third-generation Lexingtonian and seventh-generation Kentuckian, is a historian as well as a practicing attorney. A graduate of the University of North Carolina (1974, American History) and the University of Kentucky College of Law (1977), he is a founding trustee of the Lexington History Museum Inc. and now serves the museum as president and chief historian. He was named the Outstanding Citizen Lawyer by the Fayette County Bar Association in 2018. He is also a former rock-and-roll disk jockey and a retired professional soccer referee. Ockerman is the author of seven works of history, including *Historic Lexington* (2013), an anthology of his poetry and *The Ockerman Genealogical Project*, as well as numerous opinion essays. His book *The Hidden History of Horse Racing* was published by The History Press in March 2019. *A History Lover's Guide to Lexington and the Bluegrass*, which he coauthored, was released by The History Press in October 2020. He coauthored a book of photographs covering the histories of Lexington fire departments (Arcadia Press, 2021). He was also historian for the Emmy Award–winning documentary *Belle Brezing* and is host for the Emmy-nominated documentary series *Chronicles.* Foster is married to Reverend Martina Y. Ockerman (United Methodist Church). They have two daughters and two grandchildren.